Heiner Henninges   Canon EOS 1000
and Canon EOS 1000F

Canon

EOS1000 /EOS1000F

EOS REBEL / REBEL S

HOVE FOTO BOOKS — Harry Hennings

In U.S.A. and Canada
the EOS1000 and EOS1000F are known as the
REBEL and REBEL S

All text, illustrations and data apply to any one of the above cameras
USA Edition ISBN 0-906447-82-8

First English Edition June 1991
Published by Hove Foto Books
34 Church Road, Hove, Sussex BN3 2GJ

English Translation: Petra Kopp
Technical Editor: George Wakefield
Canon Technical Advice: Graham Smith
Production Editor: Georgina Fuller
Typesetting & Layout: Annida's Written Page, Sussex BN15 0NR
Printed in Germany by Kosel GmbH, Kempten

British Library Cataloguing in Publication Data
Hennings, Harry
   Canon EOS 1000.
   1. Cameras
   I. Title
   771.31

ISBN 0-906447-81-X

UK Distribution:

Newpro (UK) Ltd.
Old Sawmills Road
Faringdon, Oxon
SN7 7DS

Contents

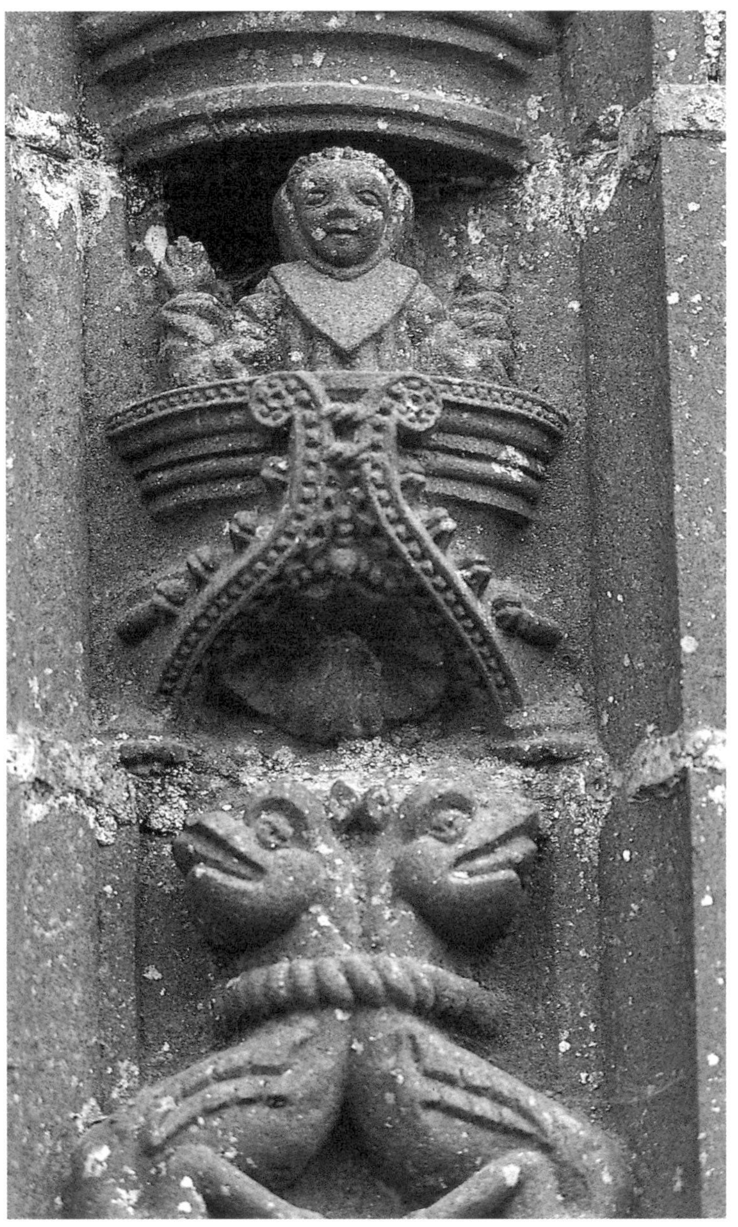

Foreword

Canon's EOS cameras have now been on the market for four years. With the EOS 1000 and EOS 1000F, or Rebel and Rebel S as they are known in USA, Canon is launching a mass campaign to widen the appeal of autofocus SLR photography. The number of components has been reduced by more than 40% by coordinating the performance levels of microchips and autofocus, a consistent building block construction method pioneered by Canon, as well as new materials from space science.

The EOS 1000 is not just a rehashed version of another EOS camera. All the important features are included. This camera is an ideal first or upgrade camera, but also an excellent second camera.

Thanks to the integral image control programs, the EOS 1000 guarantees technically perfect photographs. Moreover, the automatic control of aperture and shutter speed enables the photographer to concentrate completely on the subject.

Apart from a fully automatic program and four creative; programs for the subject areas; portrait, landscape, close-up and snapshot/sport, the Canon EOS 1000 has five further programs which enable the photographer to influence exposure.

The EOS 1000 therefore has five subject programs and five creative exposure programs, an automatic program with a program shift option, shutter-priority with automatic aperture control, aperture-priority with automatic shutter control, automatic depth of field control, as well as manual exposure. Three methods of light metering, including spot-type partial metering, guarantee optimum results for all lighting conditions. In addition to all this the Canon EOS 1000F has a built-in flash.

The lightweight combination of the EOS and the zoom lenses will prove a godsend on holiday. Even detail shots from a distance are possible with the tele zoom.

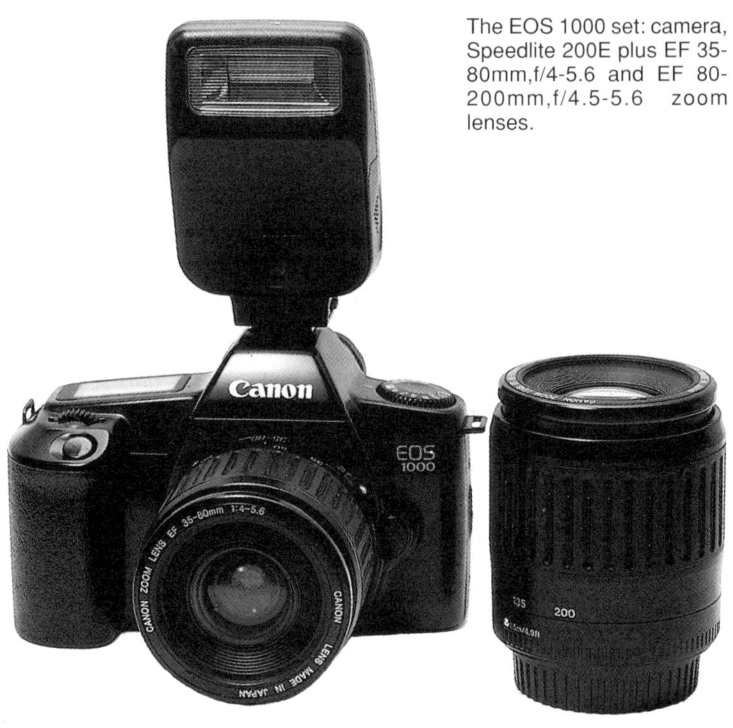

The EOS 1000 set: camera, Speedlite 200E plus EF 35-80mm,f/4-5.6 and EF 80-200mm,f/4.5-5.6 zoom lenses.

This book sets out to explain the varied technology of the EOS 1000 step by step, and to show the many possibilities of its cleverly-devised automatic programs in practice. It sets out to inform those who do not yet have an EOS 1000 about the almost unlimited possibilities of this autofocus SLR camera, and to help those who already have one to take more impressive pictures by understanding more about its technology.

The first part of the book describes in detail the camera's technology and the concepts behind it. The second part is devoted entirely to photography in practice. You'll find concrete hints and suggestions relevant to photographic tasks, which are designed to help you make maximum use of the camera's automatic programs, in order to achieve better photographs.

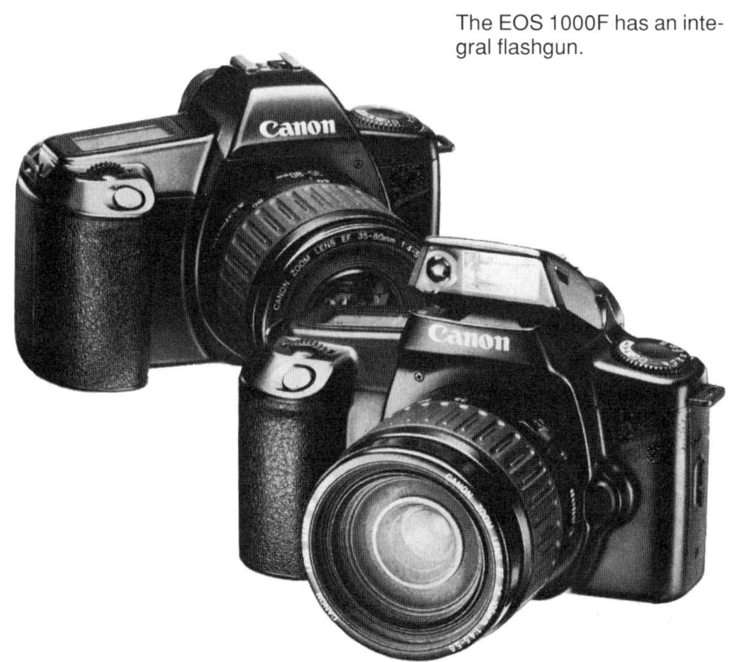

The EOS 1000F has an integral flashgun.

The third part contains a comprehensive section on subjects and information about films. It also lists the accessories from the EOS range which are compatible with the EOS 1000, and the uses of those accessories. It covers picture composition with different focal lengths as well as flash photography.

No book and no amount of theorising can replace photographic practice. So please regard the information and suggestions in this book as an invitation to collect your own practical experience. This book sets out to ease your way into photography with the EOS 1000, and to help you avoid disappointing mistakes. It describes, from the author's experience, how the EOS 1000 can be used successfully for creative photographs of high technical quality. But it also wants to show that, however automatic, it is still the photographer, not the camera, who is responsible for good photographs.

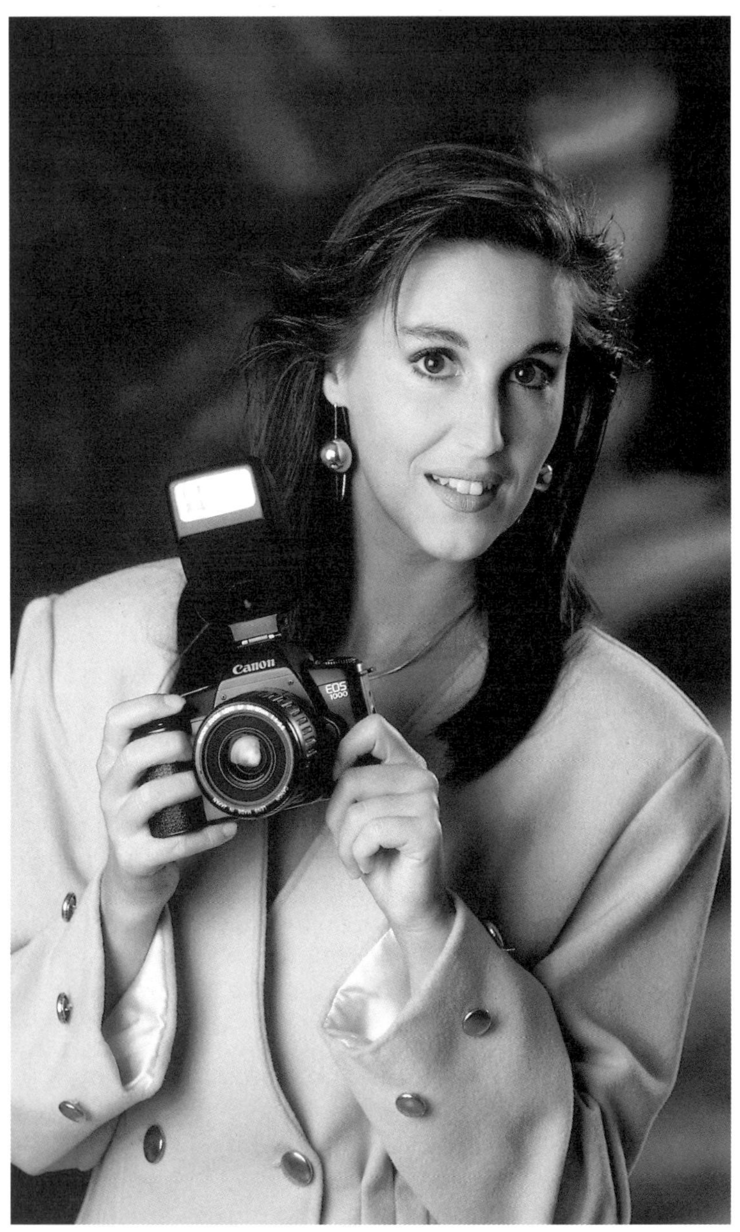

Handling the EOS 1000

Few SLR cameras will offer such simple photography with all the possibilities of an SLR system as the Canon EOS 1000 and EOS 1000F. For most subjects in the field of amateur photography it is as simple to operate as a fully automatic compact camera, but it still offers the advantage of the entire lens system of an SLR camera. The settings necessary to take a photograph are confined to a minimum. Almost all functions of the EOS 1000 are regulated by just two controls, the central command dial and the electronic input dial. All necessary function indicators can be read on the large LCD panel and, as far as necessary, also in the viewfinder. Special functions are hidden and can sometimes only be found by referring to the manual.

For snapshots and also for regular and frequent use it is important that the photographer learns to use the camera almost by touch. It is therefore a good idea firstly to familiarise yourself with the different operating elements.

Operating Elements

Central Command Dial
The command dial on top of the camera has 13 settings:
1. 'L' means 'Lock'. In this position the camera is switched off. This is symbolised by the red rectangle.
2. The green rectangle gives the go-ahead for taking photographs. It shows that automatic mode has been selected. In this program the EOS 1000 automatically regulates the two necessary

Perfect for small hands: the compact EOS 1000 together with the Speedlite 200E.

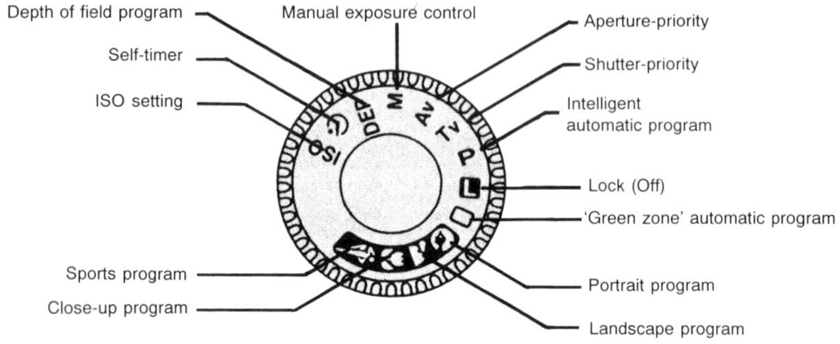

Settings on the command dial

settings, namely shutter speed and aperture. If lighting conditions are poor, the shutter speed may be too slow and could cause camera shake blur unless flash is used. This is signalled by the flashing flash symbol.

Instead of the 'green' standard program you can also choose one of the four subject programs; portrait, landscape, close-up or sport. These are fully automatic programs which take into account the creative requirements of a single subject area. The subject programs are selected simply by turning the central command dial to click on each symbol.

The shutter speed and aperture data determined by the camera and the visual autofocus signal - completion of the focusing process is also indicated by an audible signal - appear both in the viewfinder and on the LCD panel. A warning appears if the necessary shutter speed exceeds the reciprocal of the focal length used. If this is the case, the shutter speed indicator flashes continuously.

On the other side of the central command dial you will find another six exposure settings and the ISO indicator. Again, simply turn the command dial to the required setting. The symbol needs to line up with the silver mark on the camera between the command dial and the viewfinder. You can select Program AE with Program Shift (P), Shutter-priority AE (Tv), Aperture-priority AE (Av), Depth-of-Field AE (DEP), an automatic program or completely manual mode (M).

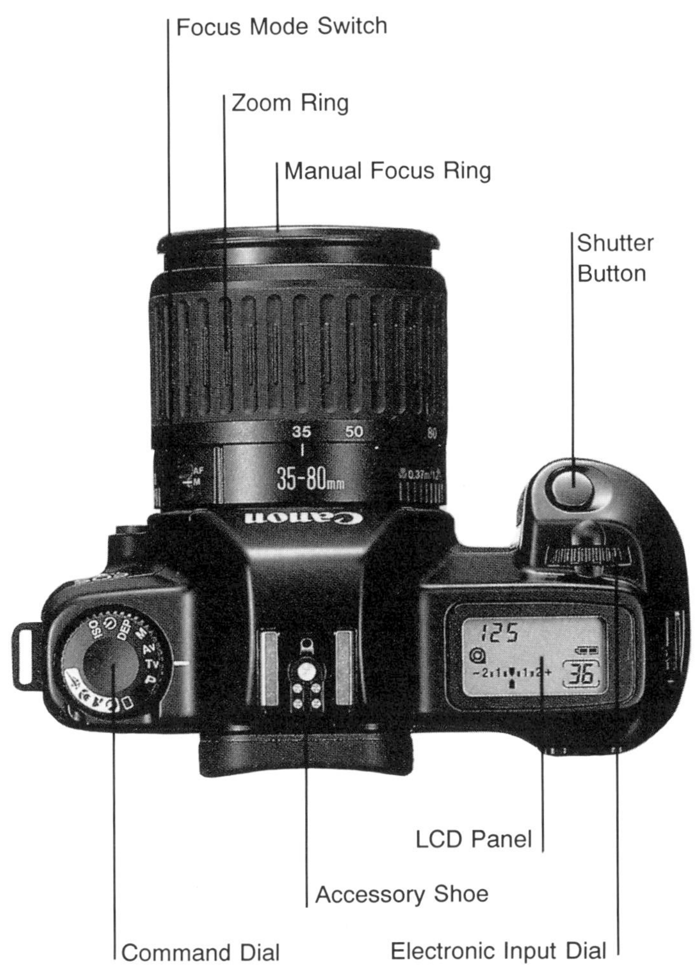

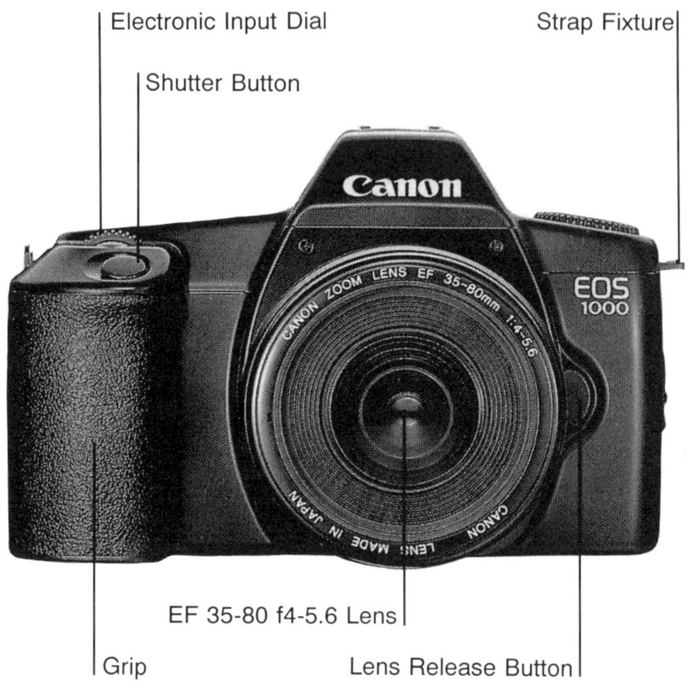

The ISO setting on the command dial, enables the photographer to select the film speed by using the electronic input dial, situated between the shutter button and the LCD panel. This is a must if the film is not DX-coded or if the film speed setting is to be deliberately altered.

Shutter Button

If the camera is switched on, the entire electronic system is activated by pressing the shutter button halfway. The autofocus system focuses on the subject; viewfinder and LCD panel indicate the selected functions. If necessary, flash is requested in the 'green zone' and 'subject' settings. The shutter button can only be pressed for exposure once focusing has taken place. The result of exposure metering is stored with the focus data if the shutter button is pressed halfway and held in position.

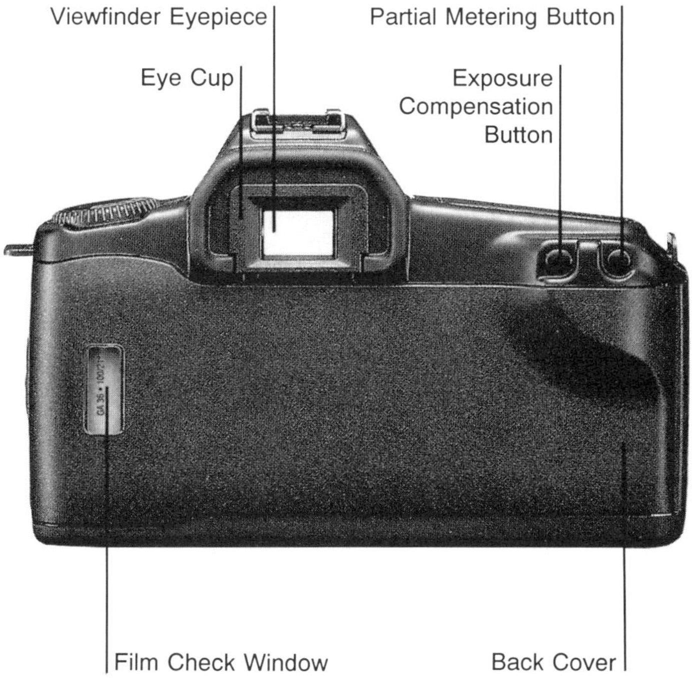

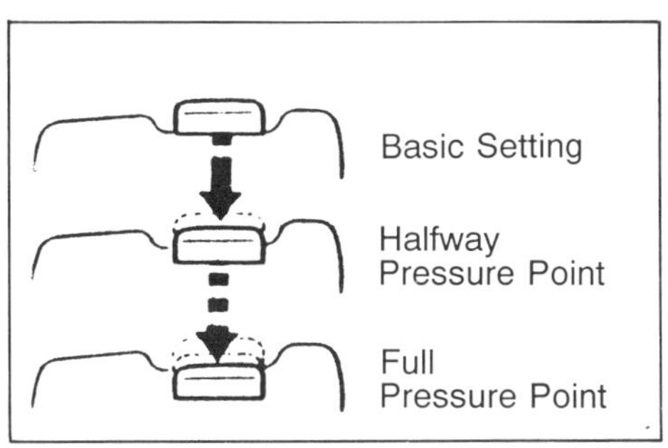

The electronic system of the camera is activated by pressing the shutter button lightly. The autofocus mechanism focuses the lens on the subject. The viewfinder and LCD panel display all functional data.

Electronic Input Dial

This component is one of the very useful elements in Canon's EOS cameras. Depending on the chosen exposure function, this dial, located directly above the shutter button, allows you to change the variable settings as determined by the function.

It can be used by itself or in conjunction with other buttons, for example the partial metering button.

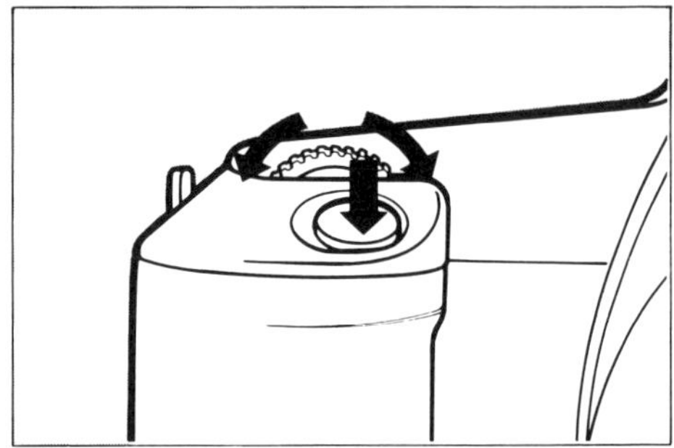

Program-specific variables are adjusted with the electronic input dial.

In the 'M' setting the electronic input dial allows variation of either the shutter speed or the aperture. To set the second variable, the aperture, you also have to press the exposure compensation button, next to the partial metering button on the back of the camera.

In the 'P' setting the electronic input dial is used to alter the combination of shutter speed and aperture selected by the camera, either to a faster shutter speed and a larger aperture, or a slower shutter speed and a smaller aperture, without changing the overall exposure.

The electronic input dial varies the shutter speed in shutter-priority mode (Tv), and the aperture in the aperture-priority mode (Av). If you are working in depth-of-field mode, the electronic input dial is used to alter the camera's chosen combination of shutter speed and aperture either to a faster shutter speed or a larger aperture.

In combination with the exposure compensation button, the electronic input dial is used to input the desired exposure compensation in half-stops between -2 and +2. Together with the partial metering button, the exposure compensation button is also responsible for multiple exposures. The desired number of exposures is selected with the electronic input dial.

Flash Button

In the 'Green Zone' setting and the subject settings a flash is 'requested', if necessary, by the flashing green symbol in the viewfinder. Often a tripod can also solve the problem. With the programs located on the other side of the 'L' on the command dial this is not possible.

The photographer must decide whether or not to use flash.

Lens Release Button

To disengage the lens from the camera, press the lens release button next to the camera bayonet and turn the lens to the left before lifting it out.

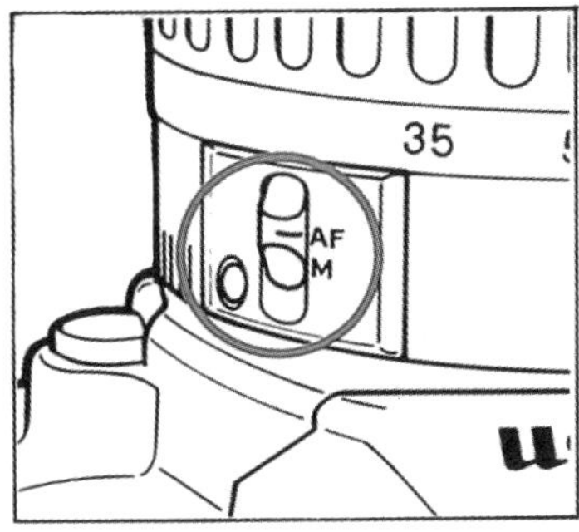

The lens release button is to the left of the bayonet. The focus mode switch on the lens has to be set to AF for automatic focusing.

Back Cover Latch

To open the back of the camera, push down the back cover latch.

Handgrip

A sliding cover lock on the underside of the handgrip opens the cover of the battery compartment.

Operating elements on the back of the camera

Partial Metering Button

The partial metering button restricts the area for light metering to approximately 9.5% of the subject area. The size of the area to be metered is indicated by the circle in the viewfinder. A green star in the viewfinder indicates that partial metering has been selected. The partial metering button cannot be used if the command dial of the Canon EOS 1000 is set on the 'green zone' or one of the subject settings.

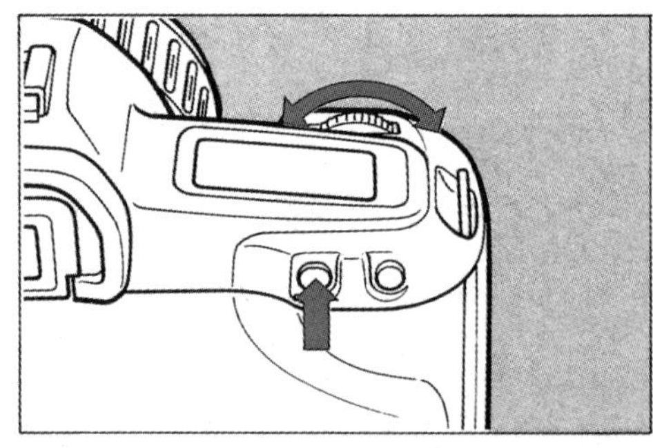

When the exposure compensation button is pressed the automatic exposure can be adjusted by +/- 2 stops, in half-stop increments, by means of the electronic input dial.

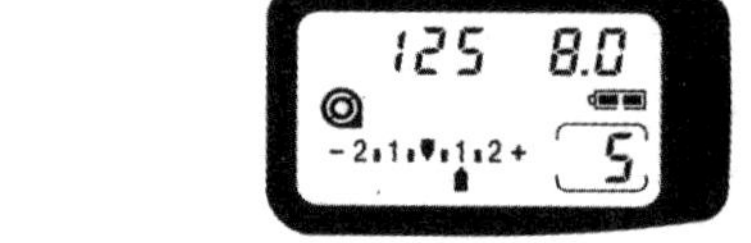

Exposure Compensation Button

If it is possible to activate the partial metering button, it is also

Close-up shots in medium reproduction ratios can be created easily with the subject setting of the EOS 1000. The main subject is clearly separated from the background because of the shallow depth of field at large reproduction scales.

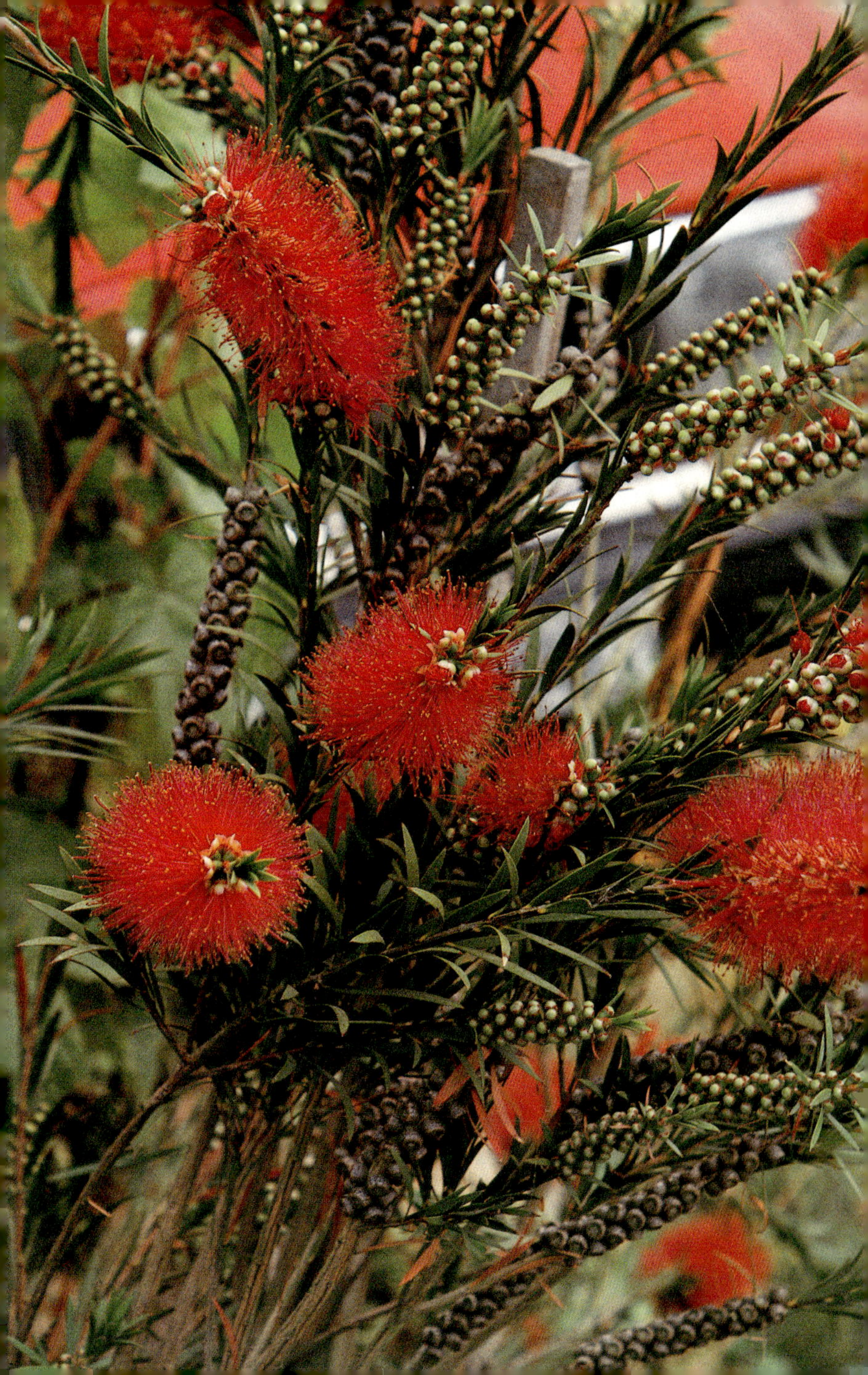

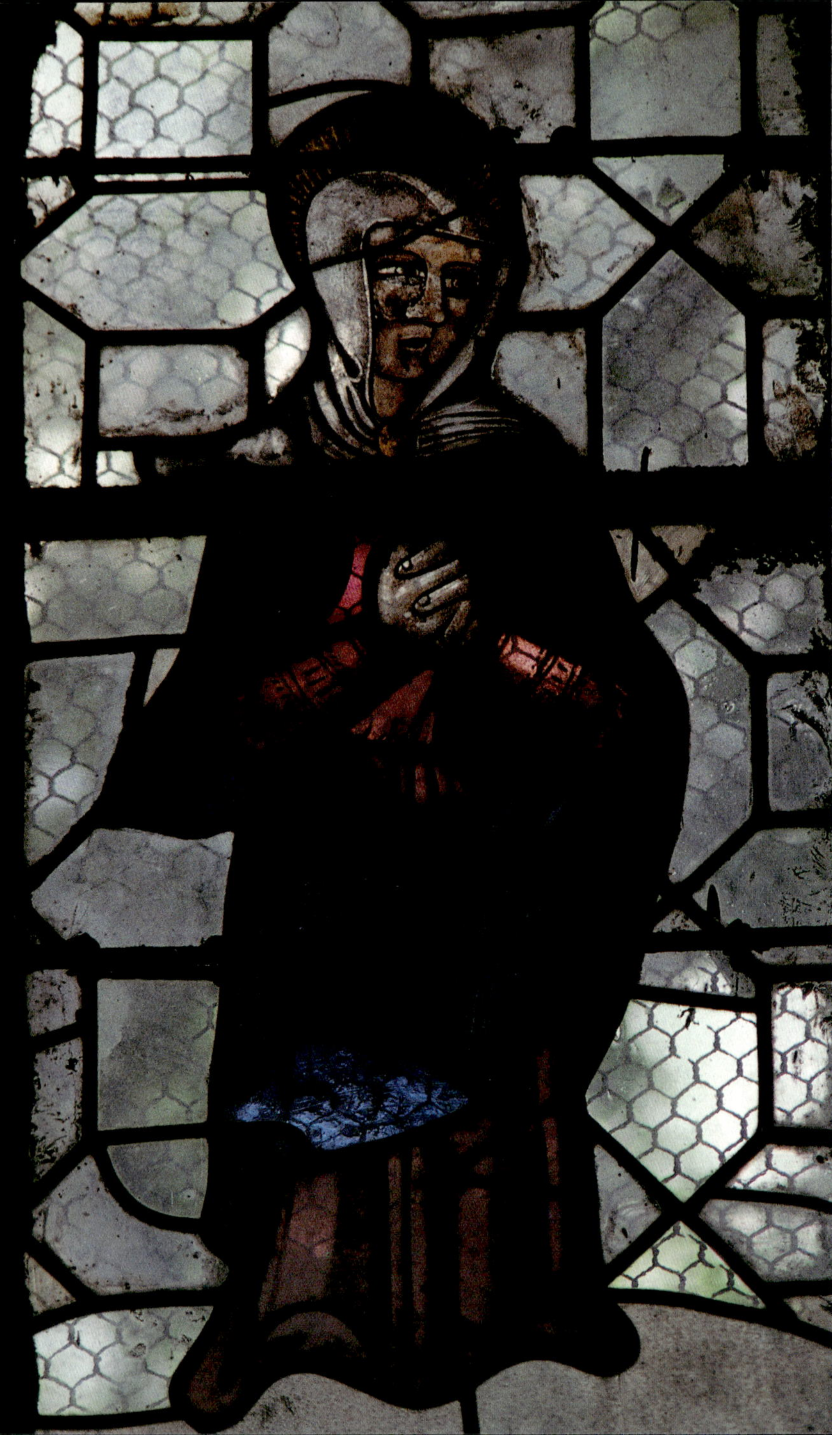

possible to use the exposure compensation button.

This is also possible in the automatic program. In manual mode, and also in 'B' mode (which signifies 'bulb'), the exposure compensation button must be pressed if the aperture is to be altered. It is used in conjunction with the partial metering button to program multiple exposure with up to nine exposures.

If the exposure compensation and partial metering buttons are pressed when there is no lens on the camera body and the command dial is set to ISO, the film is immediately rewound. This is why there is no separate rewind button.

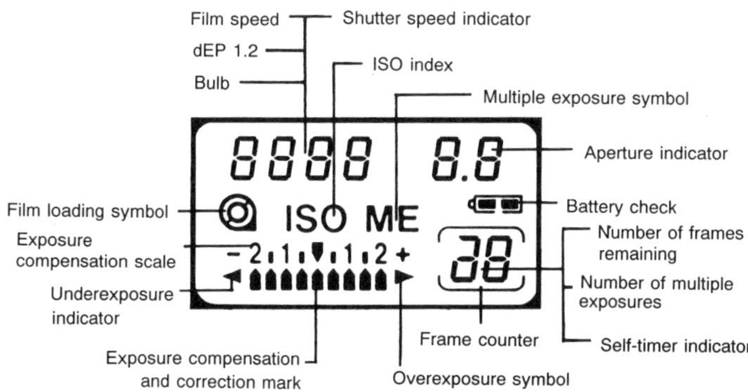

The LCD panel

LCD Panel

The LCD panel of the EOS 1000 is the camera's exterior control centre. It shows the photographer at a glance all the setting functions which are important for the creation of pictures. The panel holds a maximum of six sets of data at any one time. Which sets of data are activated on which occasions is described under each function respectively.

The three-zone metering method of the EOS 1000 effortlessly masters even backlit subjects with a lot of contrast.

The viewfinder data of the EOS 1000 is clearly arranged at the lower edge of the focusing screen. The autofocus and partial metering target areas are indicated by a square and circle respectively in the centre of the viewfinder.

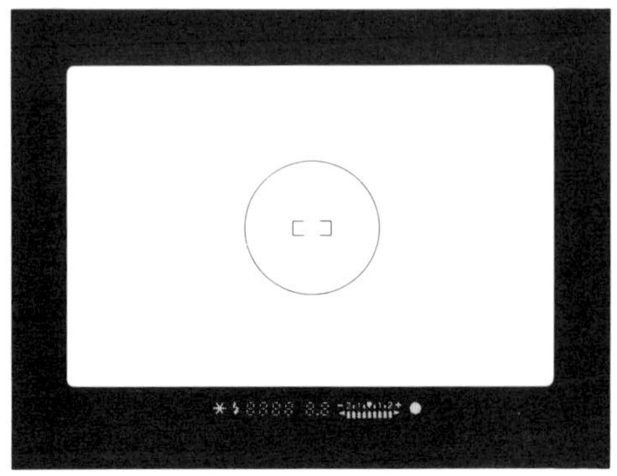

Viewfinder Data

The viewfinder data of the Canon EOS 1000 are arranged very clearly and restricted to essentials. The easily legible green LCD data are all located on the lower edge of the viewfinder. The laser-matt screen itself contains only the AF focus mark (two square brackets) and the circular partial metering area. The working methods and meanings of the activated data are described under each function.

Before You Start

Having briefly covered the component parts of the EOS 1000, it is now time to prepare the camera for taking the first photographs. This includes loading batteries and film and attaching the lens.

Battery Loading

As with all modern cameras, the EOS 1000 cannot function without power. This is why the battery must be loaded first of all before the camera is brought into service. The Canon EOS 1000 takes the now widely-used 6 V lithium battery (2CR5). Lithium batteries have the advantage of a longer life span and better resistance to temperature changes. The lithium battery provides

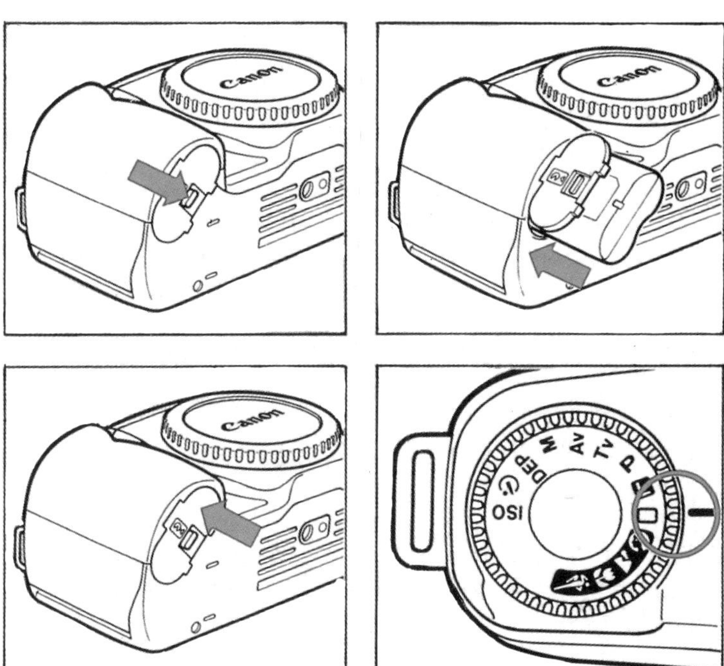

The lithium cell can be inserted into the battery compartment once the lid on the underside of the handgrip has been opened.

the entire power supply. No additional energy source is required for film transport. They are, however, considerably more expensive than the traditional alkaline batteries.

To load the battery, turn the camera upside down. Then open the cover on the bottom of the handgrip. To do this, push the small slide in the direction shown by the printed symbol until the battery cover opens. The battery can then be inserted in the compartment with the terminals facing the top of the camera.

The asymmetric shape of the battery block prevents incorrect loading. Press it lightly into the compartment, then replace the cover, pushing until it clicks shut.

When the camera is switched on, the remaining battery power is always indicated on the LCD panel at the top of the camera. Full battery power is indicated by two small black bars in the battery check symbol. If only one bar is visible, at least half the battery capacity has been used, and it is advisable to have a replacement ready.

The third version of the battery check symbol does not show a black area at all, and an immediate change is recommended. But even now the camera will still function. The camera only begins to go on strike and to stop releasing the shutter when the outline of the battery symbol starts to flash. As long as the EOS 1000 continues to release the shutter, the AF function and exposure control will work without problems. With a weak battery it is, however, possible that there is not enough power to rewind a film, and the film cassette symbol will flash. If this is the case, the battery should be changed before the camera is opened to ensure that film rewind can be completed correctly.

Compared to other autofocus cameras the EOS 1000 is modest in its use of power. It does not have an integral flash which is the largest consumer of power within a camera system. Depending on the lens used, one lithium battery can last for up to 50 films with 36 exposures each at normal temperatures. If the temperature is below zero degree, the capacity is reduced to approximately 30 films.

Naturally a lot of power is used if you constantly play around with the autofocus. The energy consumption will be higher than normal when the camera is new and the photographer does a lot of experimenting.

Attaching The Lens
The bayonet cap on the Canon EOS body is easily removed by turning it a little to the left. The same goes for the protective cover on the lens bayonet. Line up the red dot on the lens with the mark on the camera bayonet and insert the lens into the bayonet. It is locked firmly into place by turning it a little to the right until it clicks. To remove the lens, you must first press the lens release button before the lens can be turned to the left and removed.

Undamaged and clean electric contacts are important for the exchange of data between camera and lens; this is why these contacts should be protected as much as possible. You should

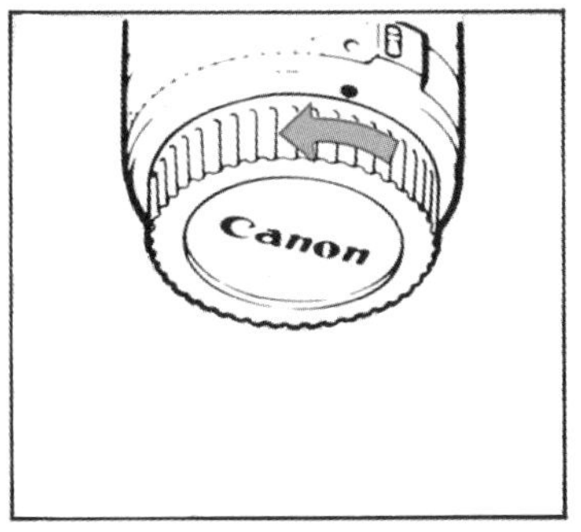

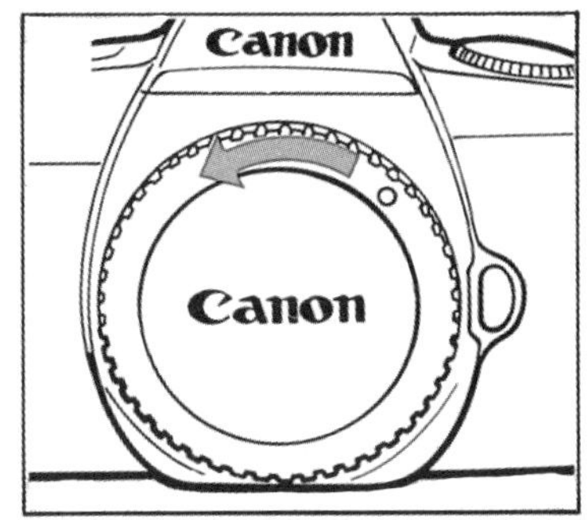

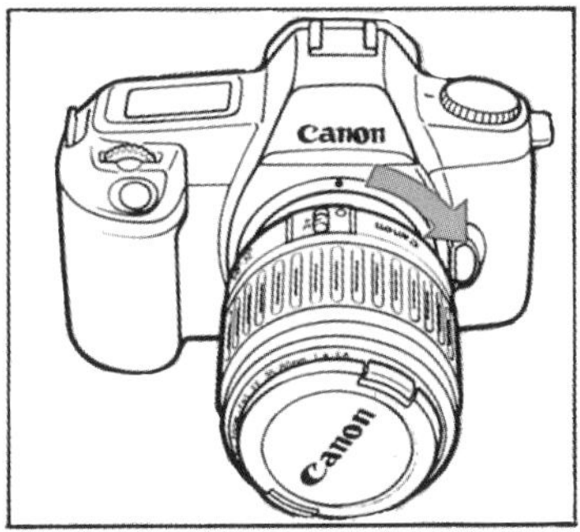

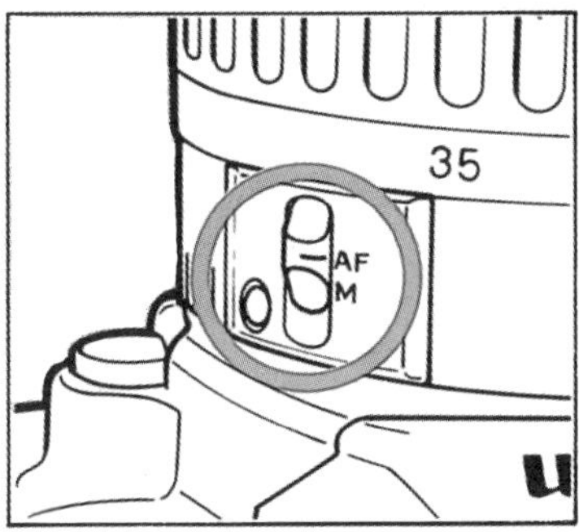

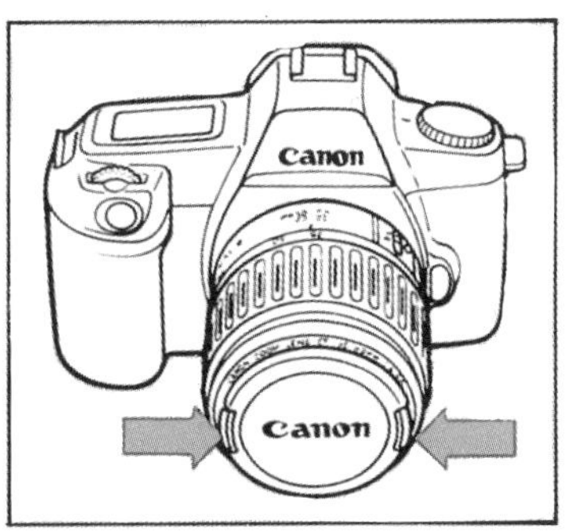

To attach the lens, the protective caps are removed from the camera and lens bayonet. The red markings are lined up, the lens placed into the camera bayonet and locked with a turn to the right. For autofocus operation the focus mode switch on the lens has to be set to AF.F

avoid touching them. Owners of other EOS cameras or lenses should not be surprised when they pick up the two special EOS 1000 lenses; instead of a shiny silvery metal ring the new lenses have a black plastic bayonet. In the opinion of Canon's technicians the polycarbonate plastics used for building aircraft are sufficiently strong to survive several thousand lens changes without any problems.

For automatic focusing the AF switch on the lens - next to the red dot - must be set at the AF position.

Film Loading

To open the camera's back cover, push down the back cover latch. The cover will spring open and the film can be loaded into the cassette compartment. The easiest way to do this is by pushing the centre of the film cassette directly onto the red locator at the bottom of the camera and then pushing the entire cassette into position. A small symbol in the cassette compartment can serve as a helpful reminder in case the cassette fails to go into the right position first time. Pull the film leader across to the red/orange mark and close the back cover by pressing it firmly. With new cameras the protective foil has to be removed from the film pressure plate before the film can be loaded. The shutter blind is a sensitive point in film loading; it must never be touched, either with your fingers or with the film leader. Its precision design is very sensitive and easily damaged.

If the camera is switched on by the main switch, or if it is already switched on, it will automatically wind the film to the last frame. The entire film is wound onto the take-up spool on the other side in approximately 10 sec. The highest frame number appears on the frame counter in a rectangle on the right-hand side of the LCD panel. With a 36 exposure film this will be 36, with a 24 exposure film 24. The first shot is therefore literally the last frame on the film and, once it is taken, it disappears into the film cassette. This is how the normal film rewind process is used to transport the film, meaning there are no long rewind times, and your photographs are safe even if the back cover is accidentally opened.

If the cassette symbol flashes after the film has been loaded and the motor has been running for a short time, it is safe to reopen the back cover, as the film has not been loaded correctly. The probable cause; the film leader was not pulled far enough across to the mark. But that is no problem and can be repeated whenever necessary. As soon as the frame number appears you can start taking photographs.

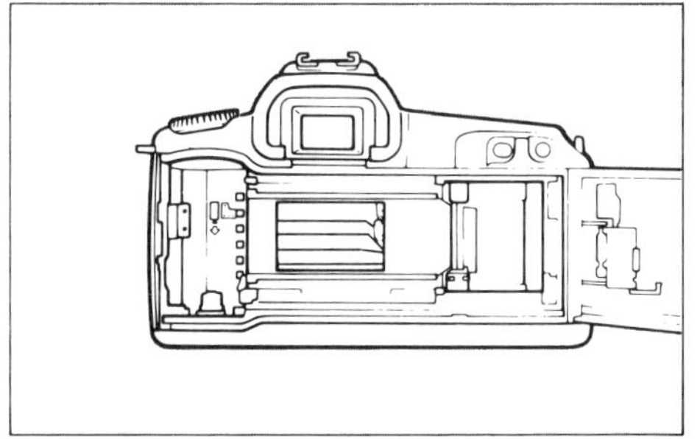

For film loading, the back cover is opened, the cassette inserted into the film compartment, and the film leader pulled across to the mark. Once the back cover is closed, the entire film is wound on.

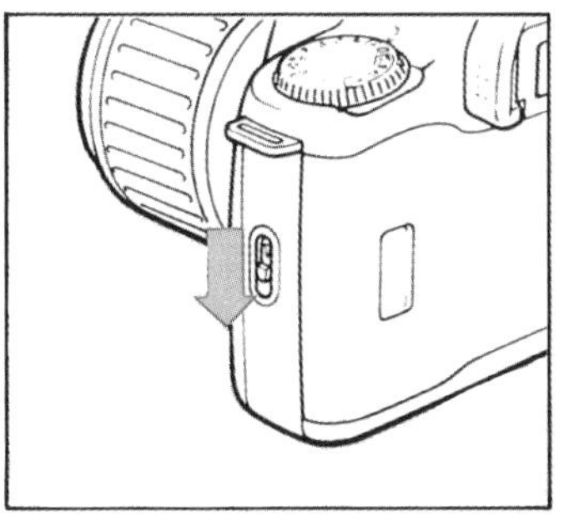

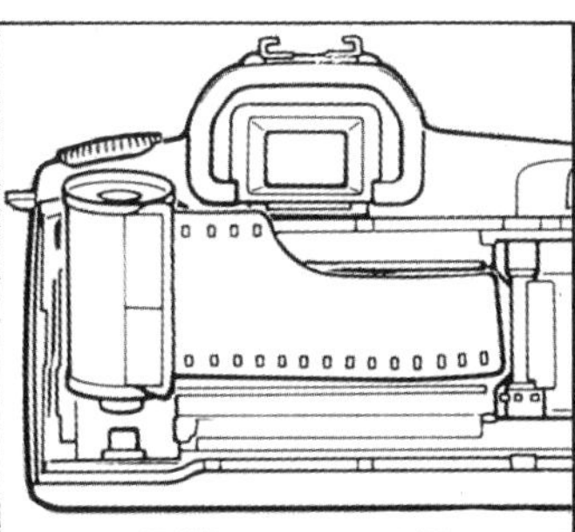

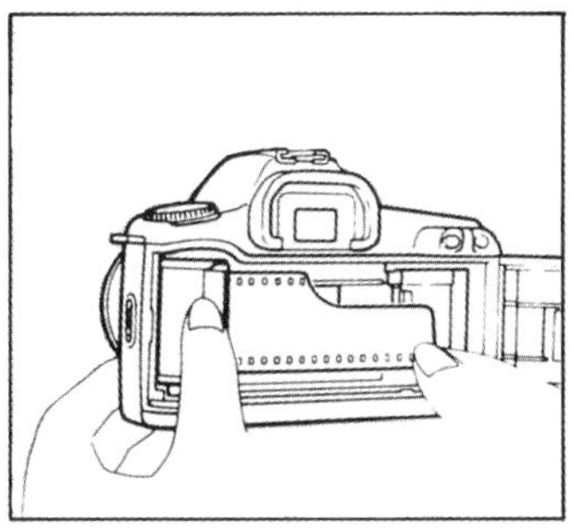

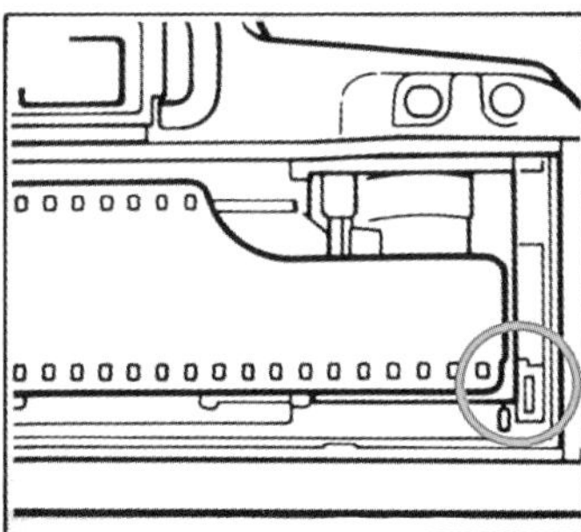

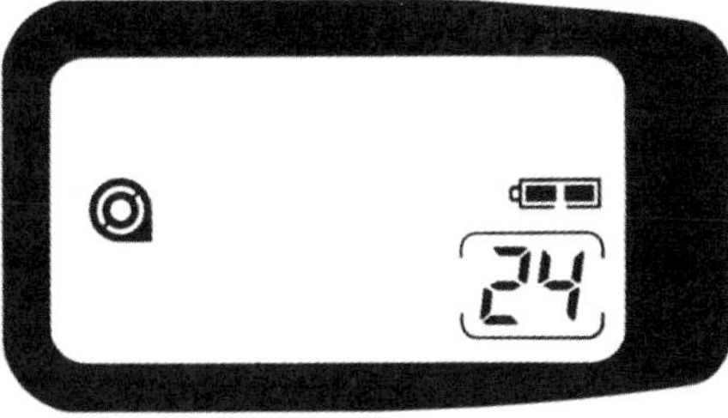

After the cassette has been inserted, correct film transport is indicated by the highest frame number.

The rewinding of a partially-used film can be activated manually at any time. As this is not a normal situation - at least for the target audience of the EOS 1000 - it is a rather complicated process. The lens must be removed, the command dial set to ISO, and both buttons on the camera back behind the LCD panel must be pressed. The rewind process will stop automatically as soon as the whole film is wound back into the cassette.

If no film is in the camera, the cassette symbol will not be visible on the LCD panel. Otherwise it is always visible, even when the camera is switched off.

Film Transport
The EOS 1000 has an integral motor for film transport. Depending on the selected program, this motor is set to single frame exposure or continuous exposure with 1 fps. Single exposure means that the shutter button must be pressed once for each shot. This applies in the 'landscape' and 'close-up' programs, the 'green zone' fully automatic and depth-of-field programs. In all other modes the camera will make continuous exposures as long as the shutter button remains pressed.

Film Speed Setting
Apart from a few exceptions, all films carry the letters DX - mostly clearly emphasised in graphics - on the actual cassette and on the packaging. This means that the film speed is coded onto the cassette and can be read by the camera. The Canon EOS 1000 can automatically set the film speed for DX-coded films in a range between ISO 25/15° and 5000/38°. The fastest material today has reached ISO 3200/36°. The ISO setting of the camera is not indicated separately. It can, however, be checked on the LCD panel by setting the command dial to ISO. If you have forgotten the ISO number, simply look through the small film window in the back cover of the camera. This is where - at least on DX-coded films - the film speed is printed on the loaded film. If the film is not DX-coded (which really only applies to specialist films and a few brands from the Eastern bloc), you can set the film speed manually with the command dial and the electronic input dial. The command dial must be set on ISO. The electronic input dial is then

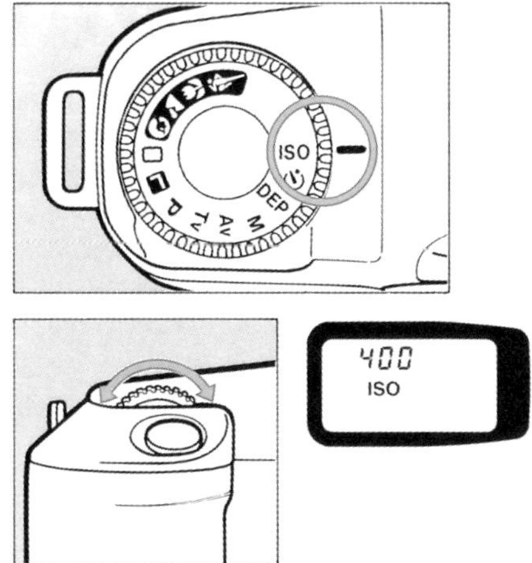

Manual film speed is selected by turning the electronic input dial after setting the command dial to 'ISO'.

turned one way or the other until the required film speed appears as the first number on the LCD panel. If no speed is set for non-DX-coded films, the setting from the previous film remains.

Manual and automatic film speed setting takes place in one-third step increments. The manual speed setting range is between ISO 6/9° and 6400/39°.

The automatically-set speed can be altered manually at any time, but any changes only remain in force until the next DX-coded film is loaded.

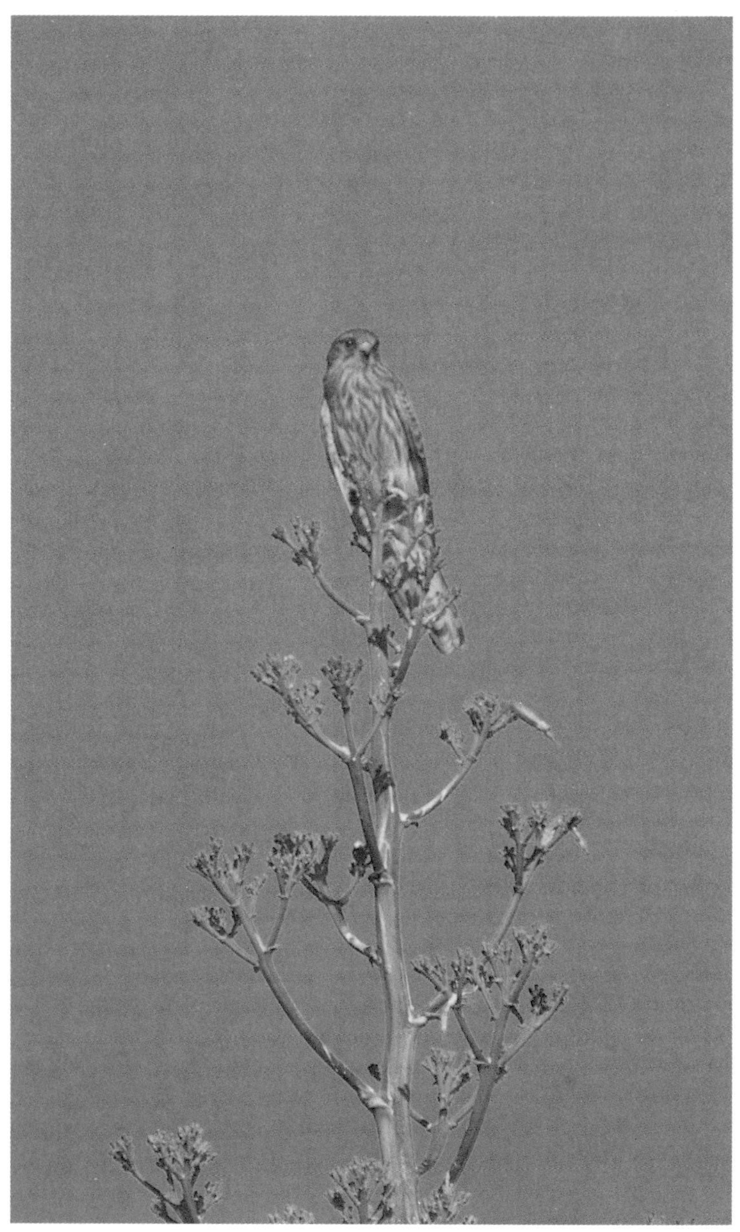

The Autofocus System

The Canon EOS 1000 uses the TTL-SIR (Through The Lens - Secondary Image Registration) focusing method. Focusing takes place on the basis of metering through the lens with a highly sensitive line image sensor. This sensor recognizes the phase shift of two part-images. The AF computer calculates the direction and amount of the lens adjustment to be carried out from the discrepancy between the part-images. The working range of the BASIS sensor (BASIS = Base Stored Image Sensor) located in the base of the camera lies between 1 and 18 EV at ISO 100/21°. This means that the EOS 1000 can focus automatically, without the help of auxiliary light, in lighting conditions as difficult as candle light. Automatic focusing in complete darkness is possible with system flash units which have an infrared AF auxiliary light. In this case, however, the range is limited to that of the auxiliary light. More about this in the chapter on flash photography.

As with all other EOS cameras, the autofocus motor is located in the lens. The two special EOS 1000 lenses boast extremely high focusing speed and precision.

The EOS 1000 shows precision in its automatic focusing in two ways; firstly in the viewfinder image, which becomes visibly sharp and clear, and secondly in the way it actually operates.

We need to distinguish between static and dynamic autofocus. As the camera chooses the operating mode itself, you need not worry about it. You only need to know that in static autofocus mode the distance measurement is stored if the shutter button remains pressed halfway. This allows you to change the composition of the photograph if required. You may wish to use this option, for example, when important details are to be used for focusing within the focus mark in the centre of the viewfinder, but

Animal shots such as this are always successful with a fast autofocus system.

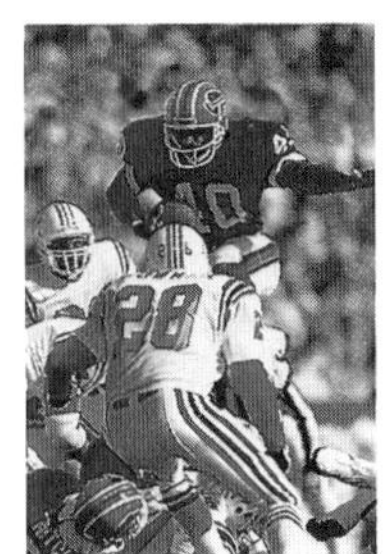 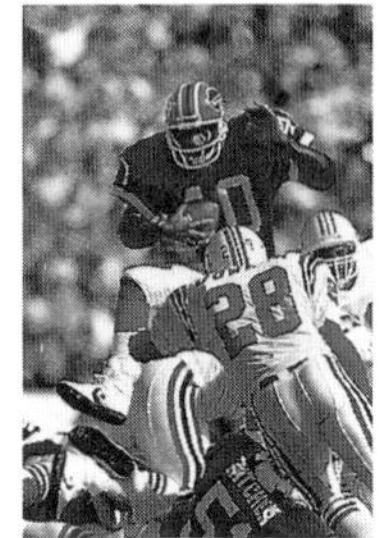 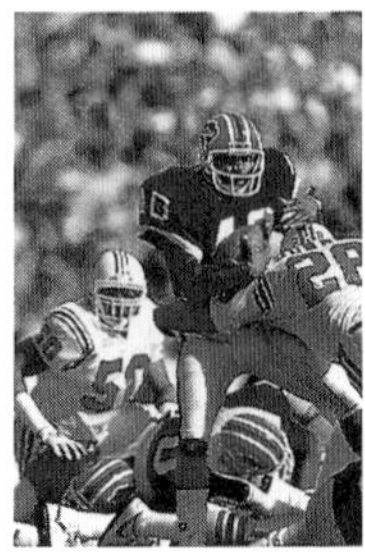

are not to be placed in the centre of the photograph. In this mode the shutter is not released until focusing has taken place.

With a moving subject the camera recognizes the movement and switches to dynamic autofocus. The result of the focusing process is not fixed but adjusted to the situation continuously. If the result were stored permanently for moving or even fast-moving subjects as it is for static subjects, complications could arise with the slight delay until the shutter is released. The subject could literally run out of focus. This is why the EOS 1000 has a mechanism which takes into account the delay between metering exposure and the actual exposure itself. And what is almost more important, the camera follows the moving subject, continuously measuring its speed and direction. It then calculates at what distance the subject will be at the point of actual exposure and focuses on that distance. All this takes place in a split second.

Moreover, you can focus manually in exceptional situations when the autofocus fails due to lack of light or low contrast.

To do this the lens switch must be set to 'M'. This really applies only in exceptional circumstances - in tests, even clear glass objects on a white cloth were focused correctly and quickly, despite the lack of contrast. With fast-moving subjects, the subject can sometimes get out of the focus range. If the camera notices this in between frames of a series, the shutter can only be released again when the fault is corrected and the subject is once again in focus.

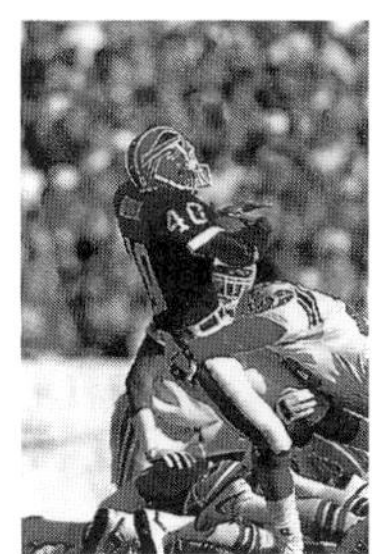 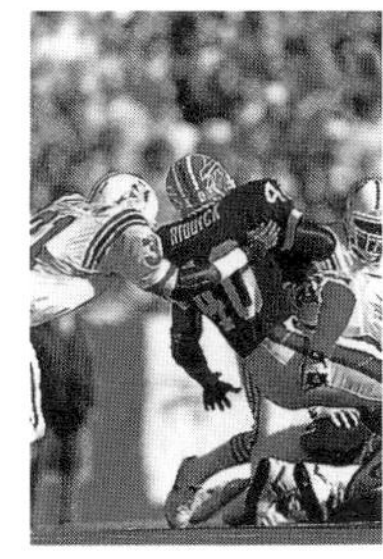

By constantly tracking the sharpness until the moment of actual exposure, the AI-SERVO autofocus makes possible super-sharp shots of moving scenes.

So you will get perfectly sharp photographs even of subjects moving quickly away from or towards the camera, despite the delay between pressing the shutter button and the moment of actual exposure.

An audible signal always confirms that focusing has been completed. The green AF indicator will flash in the viewfinder if the AF system does for once fail to focus. This could happen with special types of subjects, for example the low contrast of light-coloured areas already mentioned. Other examples are regular horizontal structures, strong backlit reflections, or objects at different distances within the AF metering area.

Often you do not have to do without the autofocus even in these situations. You can simply take a substitute measurement of a subject at the same distance, store the result until you have chosen the desired picture composition and take the picture as usual.

Manual Focusing

Manual focusing will only be necessary in exceptional circumstances. The AF switch on the lens must be set to 'M'. The metered or selected aperture and shutter speed are displayed on the LCD panel. Now turn the manual focusing ring on the lens until the subject is sharp in the viewfinder. As sharpness in the

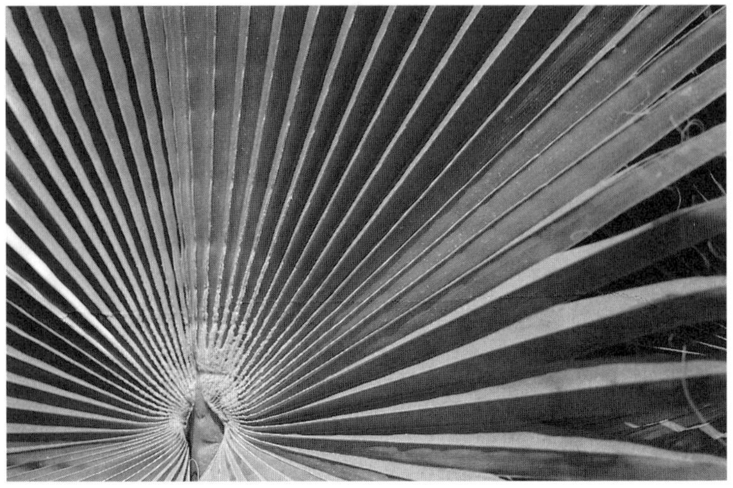

Shots like this can be achieved with the automatic close-up program without a lot of technical deliberation.

viewfinder can only be judged with experience, the LCD beneath the viewfinder continues to help by showing a green light when focusing is correct. However, not all EOS lenses can be focused manually.

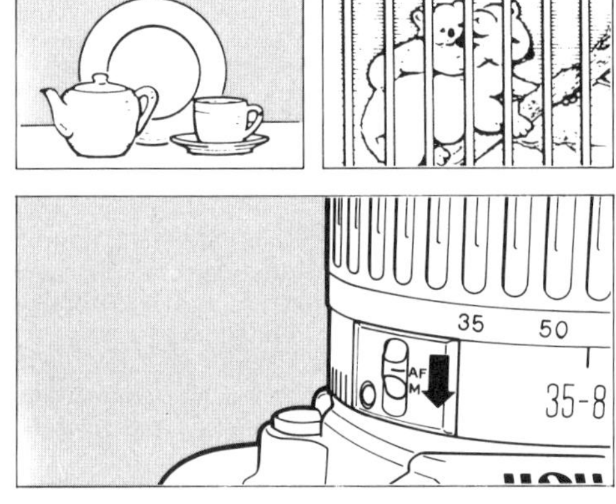

The AF system has difficulty coping with subjects with regular vertical stripes in the metering area, as well as subjects which are very reflective or have little contrast. In such cases the lens has to be switched to 'M' for manual focusing.

The Exposure Metering System

The Canon EOS 1000 has three metering methods, evaluative metering, partial metering and centre-weighted integral metering. In most cases the camera is set to evaluative metering. The other two methods are activated in just two programs, partial metering in the close-up program and centre-weighted integral metering in manual mode.

There is no metering method which can always deliver perfect results in all lighting or subject conditions. And we still need to distinguish between technically-correct or individually creative exposure. Let's take for example a backlit tree at sunset. The sun is already so weak that you can look at it directly with the naked eye. Evaluative metering will look for an exposure compromise to reproduce both the tree and the sun adequately in the shot - that is, with sufficient detail in the lightest and darkest areas of the image. The sun will inevitably lose some of its colour as it will be somewhat, if not considerably, overexposed. Until the photographer has gained sufficient experience in the different metering methods, the first shot should be taken on a standard setting. This will at least deliver an adequate and technically-correct result. For any further photographs the exposure should be determined by partial metering. To do this, press and hold the partial metering button on the back of the camera, directly underneath the LCD panel, with the thumb of your right hand. But before you do this, you have to decide where metering by this method is to take place. The area for partial metering is the circular area in the viewfinder, which is exactly 9.5% of the entire image area.

Let's return to our example. For one shot this metering area should be pointed at the sun. When the partial metering button is pressed, a green star in the viewfinder indicates that the result of this metering process is stored. Keeping the button pressed halfway, you can then choose your picture composition and take the photograph. In this case the sun will be bright red and the tree

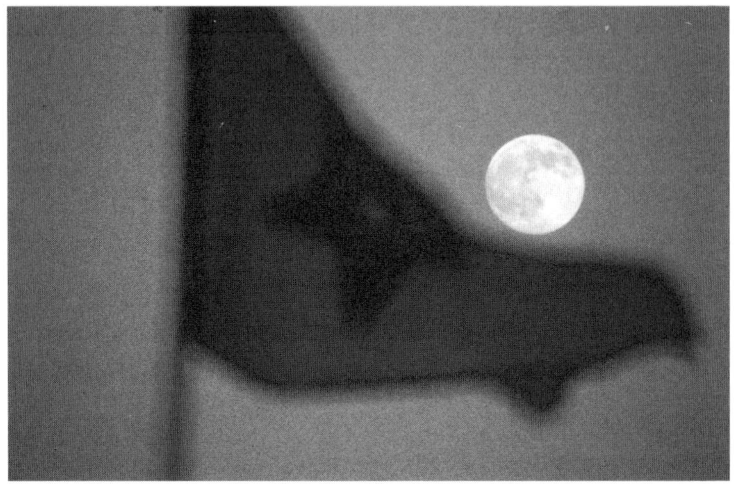

The three-zone metering system of the EOS 1000 masters even backlit subjects satisfactorily. Partial metering or manual backlight compensation is, however, advisable in strong backlight.

just an outline against a relatively dark background. The reason; the sun is the brightest part of the photograph and was on this occasion used for metering. The whole photograph will become lighter if, in a further shot, the sky - without sun - is used for metering. The result will be brighter still if the sky and part of the tree are metered. The overall result will become progressively brighter as the metering area is pointed at progressively darker parts of the subject. The partial metering button strongly influences the metering result and can therefore not be used in the 'green zone' and subject settings. In these programs shutter speed and aperture are determined according to the safest and most effective metering method for the chosen subject area. Partial metering is used only for close-ups.

The difficulties of exposure metering and control systems are not so much due to metering precision as to the analysis of the differences between light and dark subject areas. The film only has a limited exposure range, and the lightest and darkest areas of the photograph have to fall within that range so that they can be reproduced, not just in black-and-white, but with sufficient detail. Canon solve this problem on all their EOS cameras with a system of evaluative metering. It is the simplest and safest metering method for difficult lighting conditions.

Evaluative metering works with a newly developed three-zone sensor. The separate metering of three different image areas and computer-controlled analysis provide optimum results, especially in difficult lighting conditions. However, the separately-metered results are not simply used to produce an average, as many photographers used to do with multiple metering. Instead, the calculator of the EOS 1000 also compares the composition of the light/dark distribution in the image and then automatically compensates the exposure towards plus or minus. It may ask the photographer, by flashing a flash symbol, to attach and switch on a Canon Speedlite flash, in order to reach a technically-correct exposure result by filling in or completely lighting the shot.

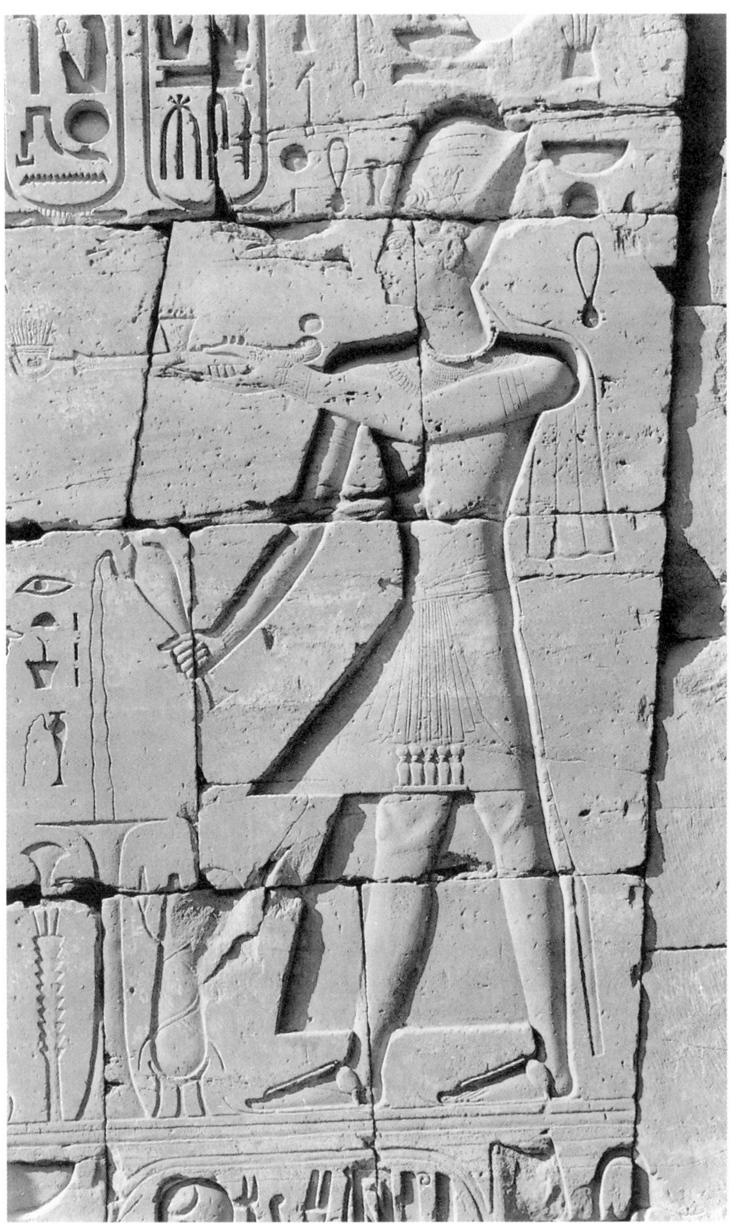

The Exposure Control System

To make sure that exposure does not remain a complete mystery, here are a few necessary technical details. Thanks to the cleverly-designed exposure metering and control systems of the EOS 1000, taking correctly-exposed photographs is no longer necessarily an art. But is correctly exposed always right? Correctly exposed means allowing exactly the right amount of light to reach a film in order to produce an image which resembles the subject as closely as possible. This applies both to the reproduction of colour and to the gradation of colour values in the light and dark areas of the image or subject.

To determine correct exposure, the intensity of the light is first measured. Even nowadays there isn't an integral exposure meter which delivers a correct result under all conditions. One of the reasons for this is that what is metered is not the light falling on the subject, but the light which is reflected by it. It is this method which has made it possible for exposure meters to be integrated into the camera in the first place. But as different parts of the subject reflect light to different degrees, the exposure meter only registers the sum of all light intensities which it regards as the average intensity according to the way it is programmed. This corresponds to a medium neutral grey. With the help of an integral computer in the camera body of the EOS 1000 this overall metering, which has been used for years, has been refashioned into a three-zone metering system. Light is metered in three different sections of the viewfinder image. The camera's computer compares this data and calculates the correct exposure from the distribution of the light intensity. It ascertains and takes into

Side or streaking light makes reliefs appear more three-dimensional.

account both the light intensity and the image contrast. This allows successful metering in complicated lighting conditions, such as backlit subjects or subjects with a light background. It also means that all recommendations regarding compensation are completely superfluous with this metering method. The only exception is partial metering of close-up shots.

With a backlit photograph, for instance, correct exposure is less important than appropriate exposure to achieve an idea for a photograph. Additional metering methods, for example partial metering, exist for this and similar tasks. Partial metering is still the most precise metering method, when used in conjunction with a telephoto lens.

Partial metering only takes into account an area in the centre of the image, covering just 9.5% of the entire image area. This area is a clearly-marked circle in the viewfinder. If you point this area at a Kodak or similar grey card in one of the 'creative zone' programs (P to self-timer), you will get a correct result for the lighting situation and for the whole shot. But the photographer must then decide whether he or she wants to, or should, for creative reasons influence the result metered in this way. This is done by pressing the exposure compensation button (next to the partial metering button on the back of the camera) and turning the electronic input dial. The amount and nature of the compensation, whether plus or minus, is displayed on the LCD panel and in the viewfinder. The compensation takes place in half stops.

As we saw in the example of the sunset, there are situations when the photographer may wish to influence the final result by determining the metering area himself, deviating from the 18% reference figure. The crux of creative photography is often the best possible amount of light for the realisation of an idea of a photograph, regulated via aperture and shutter speed. Aperture

Quick snapshots, such as this of an idyllic fellaheen settlement on the bank of the Nile, succeed without lengthy preparation in the 'green zone' program.

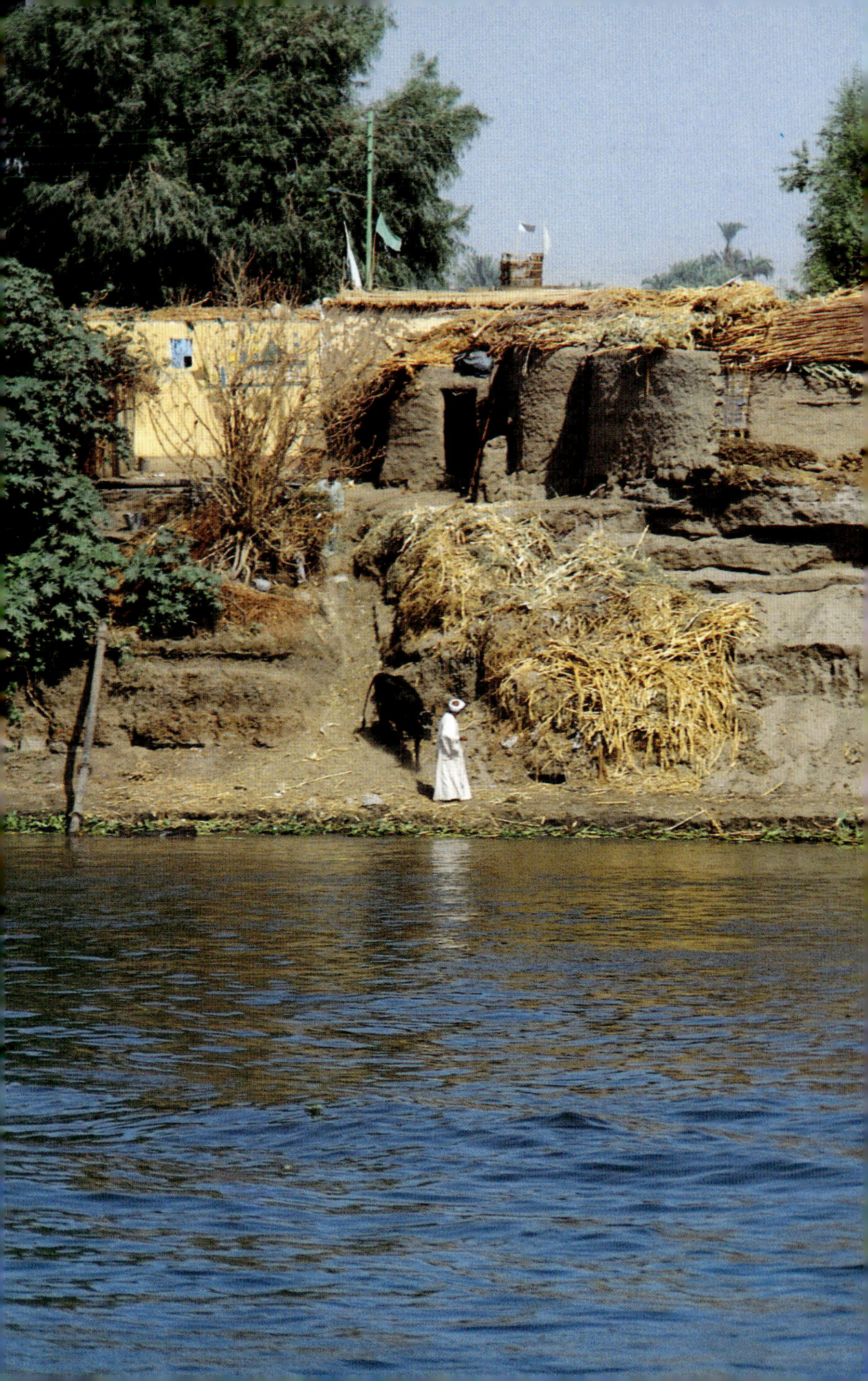

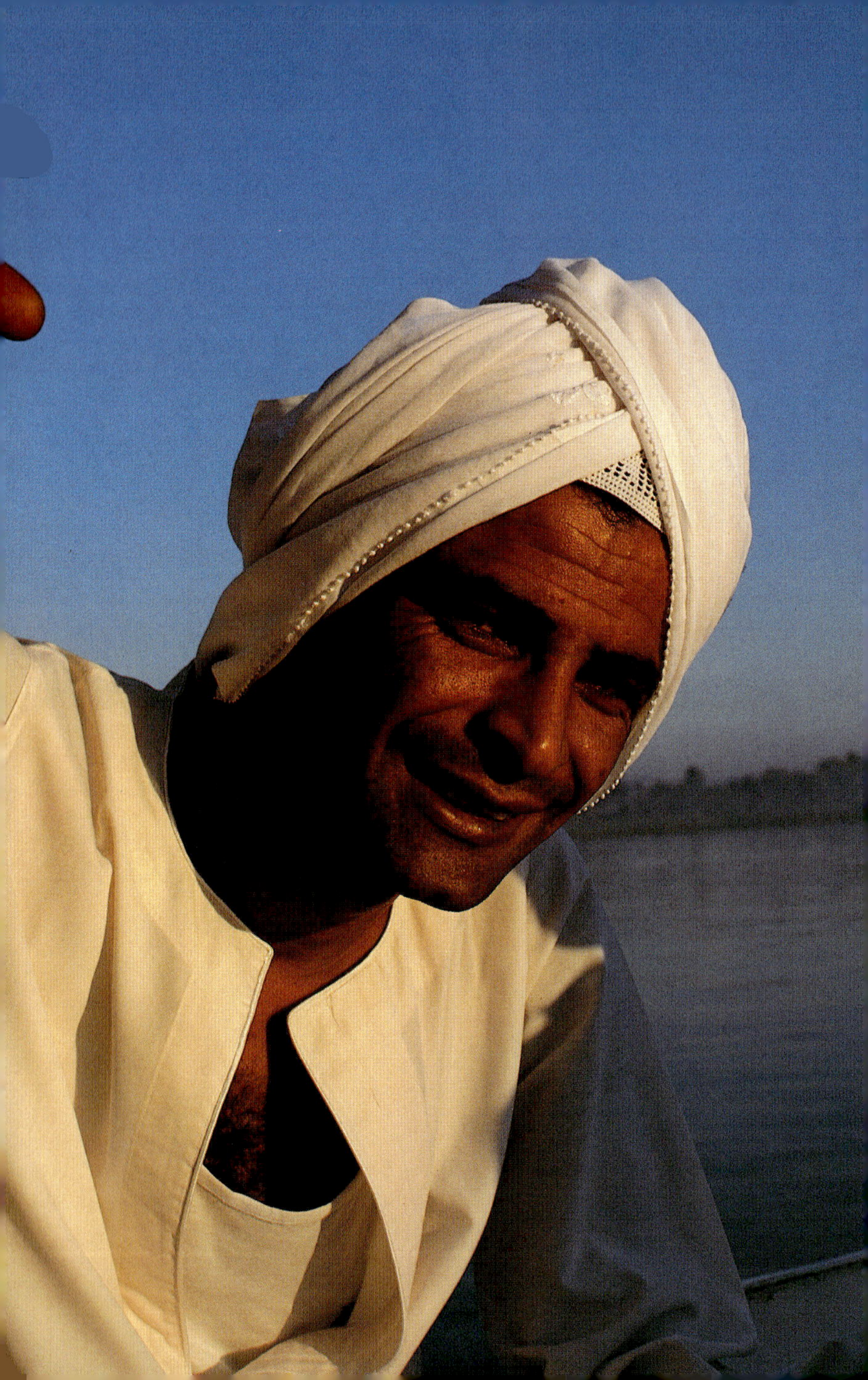

and shutter speed in themselves are important creative elements. The EOS 1000 therefore offers many different exposure programs to allow you to employ aperture and shutter speed creatively - either together or separately - according to your own ideas, while always giving correct exposures.

P - fully automatic - everything is done for you, but you can make changes if you wish;

Tv - Shutter-priority - you choose the shutter speed, the aperture is determined automatically;

Av - Aperture-priority - you choose the aperture, the shutter speed is determined automatically;

M - you choose shutter speed and aperture, freely or according to exposure meter data;

DEP - Depth-of-field program - you choose the zone for depth of field by setting focus points, shutter speed and aperture are determined automatically.

A further fully-automatic program with a clock for its symbol is known as self-timer. The shutter is not released until 10 sec have elapsed after the shutter button has been pressed.

To take the best possible photographs with these programs, found on one side of the command dial, you need to have at least a basic knowledge of photography. But there are plenty of situations, covering probably more than 80% of amateur photography, which can be grouped into just a few areas. Each of these areas has its own photographic rules, and its own similar technical

---

conditions. This is why Canon has developed a separate exposure program for each of these subject areas. The secret of these settings is subject-specific camera control, which substantially improves not just the technical quality of many photographs but can also help to promote the photographer's creativity.

This gives even photographers who do not concern themselves greatly with technique the opportunity to concentrate fully on the creative aspects of photography, and to leave technique mostly to the camera. This has proved very successful with other EOS cameras.

Subject Settings

The photographer can easily determine whether the camera is to operate in an uncomplicated automatic program suitable for the subject, or whether it is to serve as a creative tool - it just takes a single turn of the central command dial.

The black L (Lock) in the red square blocks all functions, the LCD panel does not show any symbols, the camera is electronically switched off. It is activated with a small turn to the left or right. But even this turn must be deliberate, for it decides how much or how little technique the photographer wishes to use.

Very little technique is needed if the photographer turns the command dial towards the 'green zone', or further to one of the subject settings. Canon's subject settings are also known as the PIC-system (Programmed Image Control), and the four programs control automatically all the important camera functions in a way which is surprisingly practical. These programs are ideal for carefree photography, and for the amateur photographer who does not want to practise the more advanced photographic skills every day, but who still demands optimum results. The subject settings are: 'Green Zone' Portrait, Landscape Close-up, Sport.

Clearly recognisable symbols on the command dial assist in the choice of setting. Once the dial has been turned to one of these symbols, the steps for taking the picture are reduced to a minimum for the photographer:- recognize the subject, decide on the composition, press the shutter button. The camera chooses the

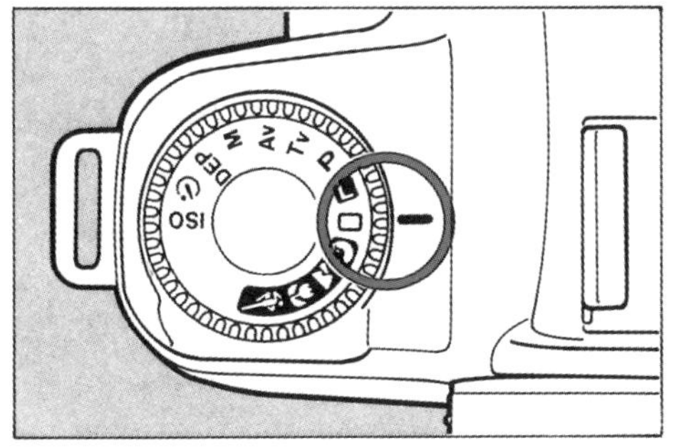

Easily-understood symbols on the command dial of the EOS 1000 mark the subject settings for portrait, landscape, close-up and sports shots.

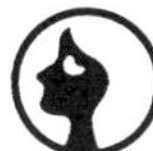   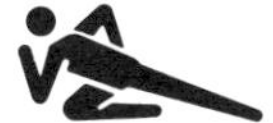

ideal automatic focus, the most successful exposure metering method and method of film transport - everything is done automatically in such a way as to be suitable for the subject setting. Direct interference, such as switching to partial metering or manual exposure compensation, is no longer possible, but also no longer sensible.

The 'Green Zone' Program

When you're driving, green signals means 'go', and the green rectangle on the central command dial of the EOS 1000 has exactly the same task. It marks the standard program, the automatic program. Technically it is identical to the other P-program marked on the creative side of the central command dial. Depending on the focal length of the attached lens, the camera chooses the most suitable combination of shutter speed and aperture.

With this green light for instant photography you can probably capture perfectly more than 80% of all normal subjects. Canon describes the 'green zone' program as an 'intelligent automatic program'. This means that when there is little light, the program operates in aperture-priority. It takes the photograph with the widest possible aperture; between f/4.5 and f/5.6 with the standard EOS 1000 zoom lens. The exact figure depends on the chosen

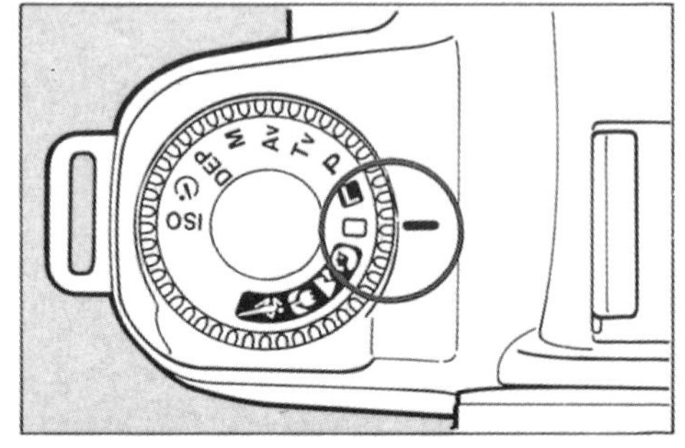

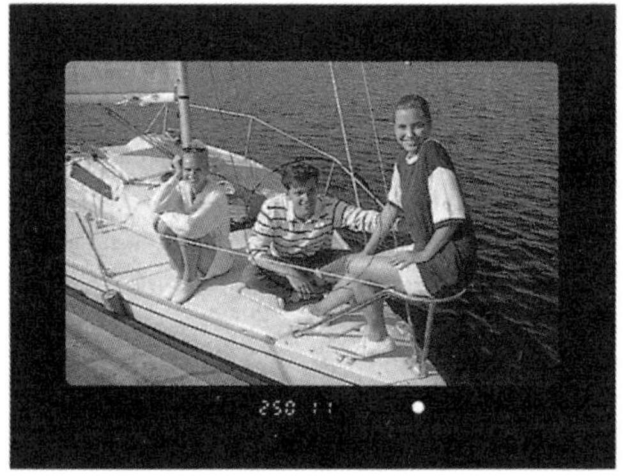

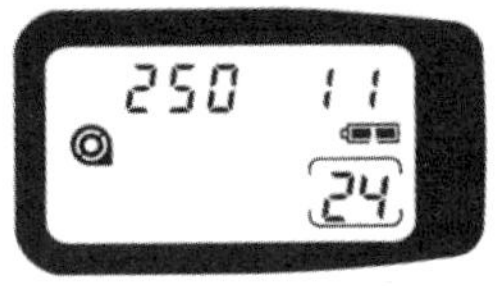

focal length, which also determines the image scale. It is in any case displayed beneath the viewfinder and on the LCD panel. The flash symbol and the metered shutter speed will flash if the largest aperture demands a shutter speed which is slower than the reciprocal of the chosen focal length in mm. The photographer is advised to attach a flash, an EOS Speedlite, to the accessory shoe and switch it on. If for some reason this is not possible, the camera should be put on a tripod. Otherwise there is a distinct danger of camera shake blur because the shutter speed is too slow. The automatic program will only start if, with the widest aperture, a shutter speed is reached which is faster than the reciprocal of the focal length. Normally the flash symbol and the indicated shutter speed will then stop flashing, the camera will stop down the aperture and at the same time reduce the shutter speed. Shutter speed and aperture change at the same pace. However, the intelligence of the program lies not in this process, which is an international standard, but in the information which, for example, a zoom lens feeds into the camera; its focal length range (initial and final focal length) as well as the maximum aperture corresponding to the selected focal length. This means that the exposure program is optimized several times, and when the focal length of a zoom lens is changed, the program adjusts to the new focal length as many as five times, though usually only twice.

The reciprocal of the focal length is regarded as the limit for the slowest possible shutter speed for hand-held photographs without the danger of camera shake blur. At slower shutter speeds in the 'green zone' and all subject settings, the flashing shutter speed serves as a visual warning signal for camera shake. A warning signal to be taken very seriously, for if you still get unsharp photographs even with an EOS 1000, it will mostly be due to camera shake. Another source of mistake is lenses which were set to manual and have not been switched over. So watch out for the green dot and the audible automatic focus signal.

When the shutter button is pressed halfway, focusing takes place first. The system itself decides which autofocus method is to be used, and this is also retained for any subsequent photographs. The shutter mechanism is only released when focusing has taken place.

A green flash symbol will flash in the viewfinder in backlit conditions, or when there is insufficient light to avoid camera shake. If the flash is ready, the green flash symbol is lit permanently. The shutter release process can only be controlled and stopped by the flash in very bad lighting conditions, when the autofocus can no longer function and is waiting for the infrared auxiliary light from the flashgun. In the 'green zone' program, film transport is set to single frame, and the shutter button must be released and then pressed again for every subsequent shot. The analytical evaluative metering system ensures correct exposure, even for extreme subjects such as snow in sunshine.

'Green zone' is a program for standard subjects, uncomplicated snapshots and souvenir photographs without much creative thought. If you're not sure which program to choose, this one guarantees to deliver a high percentage of successful photographs, regardless of the focal length. So you can use the whole range of EOS lenses to their full potential.

The Portrait Program 

This program is designed for the use of longer focal lengths. For zoom lenses the longest focal length is recommended. This is 80mm for the 35-80mm standard zoom, whereas all focal lengths are possible on the 80-200mm zoom. For classical portraits a focal length between 90mm and 135mm is generally considered suitable.

The program is tailored for two typical portrait styles; the one best known as a passport photograph, and the other where the face almost fills the frame.

If you get so close to your subject that the head and shoulders fill the frame in the viewfinder, you should point the focus mark at the eyes, press the shutter button halfway and hold it there and press down completely when you have found the image framing you want.

This is essential, otherwise the base of the neck is often extra sharp, but not the eyes, which always most clearly express personality. This also means that the focus area has to be revised and refocused after every photograph. This exposure program is designed to provide a selective area of focus by setting a comparatively large aperture. Selective focus therefore has the advantage of guiding the eye to the essential and dissolving even busy backgrounds into pleasant unsharpness. This is, of course, impossible if the person is very close to the background. Therefore it is important that the distance between subject and background should be as large as possible, and the smaller the subject appears in the shot, the larger this distance should be. If the face is almost

50

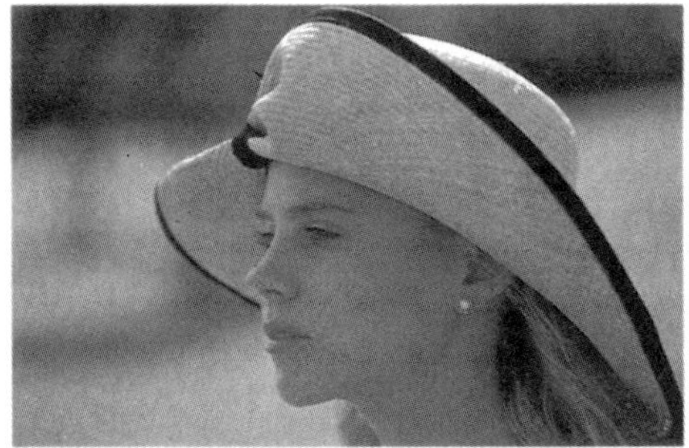

The portrait program of the EOS 1000: the easiest way of taking good portrait shots.

to fill the frame, the background need only be a metre away in order not to appear intrusive. As a rule of thumb, the distance between subject and background should be not less than a third of that between the camera and the subject. But more is never wrong.

In this program the camera stores the established focus and will use it for further photographs until you take your finger off the shutter button. The continuous exposure mode in the portrait program is designed to help capture changes in facial expression.

In strongly backlit conditions, or when there is too little light, this program suggests a flash by giving the visual flash signal in the viewfinder. Exposure metering in the portrait program takes place by evaluative metering and does, of course, take into account an attached flash.

The Landscape Program

This subject setting is programmed for one shot autofocus and single frame exposure. This is self-evident, as things are rarely hectic with landscape subjects. Furthermore, there will always be time to press the shutter button a second time.

The manual recommends: use a wide-angle lens or the wide-angle setting on your zoom lens, to create a feeling of space and depth. Photographically this is just one of several solutions for good landscape shots, but it is one which is consistent in the landscape program. The analysis of many thousand landscape shots has shown that nature subjects are often found very near infinity. For the amateur photographer landscapes almost always take the form of a panorama. And if you want to have a lot in your photograph, you will, of course, want it in focus from front to back. This is why the program ensures an adequate depth of field by selecting a small aperture. So you will not be surprised at the advice to use the 35-80mm zoom lens only at its shortest focal length of 35mm, or to use other lenses with even shorter focal lengths, in order to fit even more of the subject in the shot. If you want to capture sections of the landscape in front of you with a telephoto lens or with focal lengths above 50mm, you should switch to the 'green zone' program or, if you're prone to camera shake, even select the snapshot or sport program.

You can assume that in the circumstances just described, the landscape program can turn more than 90% of landscape subjects into clean, correctly-exposed photographs with impressive depth of field. Extreme wide-angle lenses - with a focal length below 28mm - are difficult for composing pictures. They demand considerable experience if the foreground, and later the viewer's reaction, is not to be predominantly empty.

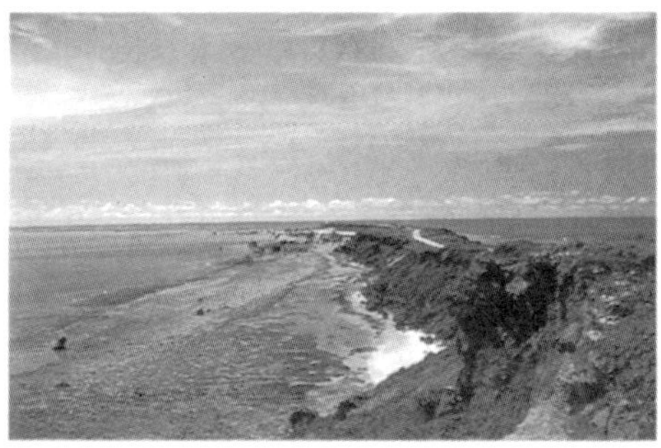

The landscape program automatically selects the correct aperture to achieve the necessary depth of field.

The Close-up Program 🌷

In this subject area the photographer will quickly reach the limits of the light or, more precisely, the limits of sufficient light intensity. This is why the close-up program is designed for photographs with continuous artificial light sources, as well as flash. You can, of course, attach any Canon Speedlite to the accessory shoe. The advantage of flash is that the electronics of the camera and the flash are compatible and can therefore be coordinated precisely. The flash often takes on the task of filling-in and only becomes the main light source if there is a lack of light. This program prefers moderate apertures in order to extend the small depth of field intrinsic in this subject area while retaining shutter speeds suitable for hand-held shots.

Without an additional flash, this program runs in the same way as the landscape program. However, whereas depth of field is used in the infinity area in the latter, this uses it in close-up.

Let me emphasise that depth of field remains constant if the aperture and size of the image also remain constant. The only thing that changes in the photograph is the size of the image in relation to the background, and therefore the unsharpness of the background. If you understand this rule and do not frequently try to get as close as possible with your telephoto and zoom lenses, thereby using them at minimum distance, you will miss out on many a feeling of achievement with extraordinary shots. To ensure the best possible exposure for all subject details, the program switches to partial metering when no flash is used. The metering area corresponds to the circular area around the focus mark in the viewfinder. While the shutter button remains pressed halfway, the close-up program stores the focus and exposure data. With very light or very dark details in the centre of the subject, colour values can sometimes deviate from the original in this program. Very light colours can become darker, dark ones lighter. If you want to reduce this to a minimum, aim at a green area (if possible at exactly the same distance as your subject) and hold the shutter button halfway.

The two special EOS 1000 zoom lenses can be recommended for this program - both of them have an interesting shortest focusing distance.

Set at 80mm, a distance of exactly 37cm (from subject to back edge of the LCD panel) you can record a subject area the size of a postcard or the operating manual. Set at 35mm, the same distance covers a subject area approximately A3 size.

Although the EOS 1000 lenses and some other zoom lenses can focus at short distances, this does not replace a macro lens. These

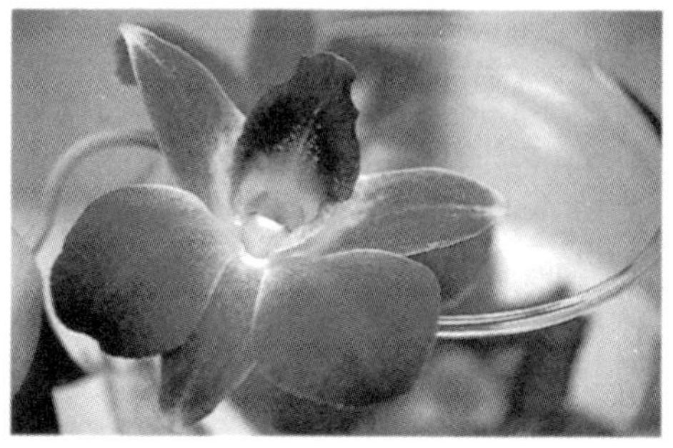

shots rely on sharpness at the centre of the image and necessitate a sufficient reduction in aperture, which takes place automatically in this close-up program.

But with close-up photographs you have to take into account further considerations. At a distance of 37cm, with the small zoom lens set at 80mm, the depth of field area is barely 5mm with the largest aperture, and not even 4cm with the smallest aperture. Everything within these ranges are recorded as acceptably sharp.

A clever choice of subject area cannot get around the problems of a small depth of field altogether, but it can reduce them to an acceptable degree. With flowers, for example, align their largest part parallel to the film plane. This transfers the small depth of field to the largest possible area.

They are best photographed directly from above or from the side, so that the largest area is always parallel to the film plane. If you want to photograph them any other way, you should aim to keep the loss of sharpness as inconspicuous as possible and in the background.

Snapshots and Sports Photography 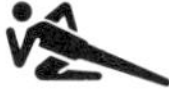

Even beginners can achieve convincing sports photographs with the sports program - if they can get close enough to the subject and can get it to more or less fill the frame. But the program can also give extra sharpness to normal holiday or family subjects, especially where fast movement is involved. If you want to capture your subjects quickly and simply, the sports program is ideal for snapshots. This program is suitable both for life-like snapshots of children, pets and hobbies and for scenes with movement, for example the activities in a market.

Children are a typical subject for this program. It could be a photograph of your daughter's first attempt at galloping in a pony race or your son with his racing bike, or hundreds of other similar family subjects. As an amateur photographer you don't need a big sports festival or a world cup match in order to take technically-perfect photographs in the sports program. The same technique is required for junior's first jump off the one-metre board in the swimming pool, or his ball practice to fulfil his ambition of becoming a famous goalkeeper. The sports program can capture everything, filling the frame with a sharp image. But note the word 'can'! If you go to the Monte Carlo grand prix without experimenting with the sports program beforehand, don't be surprised if it doesn't work quite as you'd imagined.

You can't expect to take 36 sharp and spectacular photographs by pulling out your camera at the last moment, probably with a 200mm telephoto lens, and just pressing the shutter button. You should be familiar with the highlights of any particular sport, get close enough - which often means using focal lengths longer than 300mm - and the program will reduce photographic technique to simply releasing the shutter. The program sequence shouldn't endanger success; the emphasis is on fast shutter speeds but not at the expense of apertures that give a moderate depth of field. Movement is to be frozen and therefore reproduced clearly and sharply. If there is sufficient light, the shutter speed is increased first - by a maximum of three steps. These fractions of a second are then reduced by a further three steps. With the 80-200mm lens this is $^1/_{200}$ sec plus three steps; the shutter speed ranges from $^1/_{200}$ sec to $^1/_{1600}$ sec. The program only begins to reduce the aperture rather than further increasing the shutter speed when, with sufficient subject brightness, the reciprocal is reached. This type of exposure control is very practical, especially in the

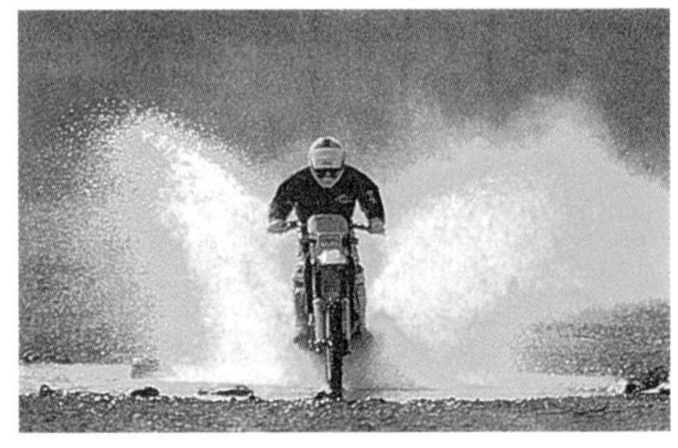

telephoto range above 200mm. By starting a series relatively early, you allow the autofocus to recognize the approaching movement, not just in time but early, so that it can calculate exactly where the subject will be at the point of shutter release and at the next point of metering. You will get sharp pictures, even of fast-moving subjects, from the first to the last frame. At least this applies for that part of the subject which is within the depth of field. At a distance of 10m and an aperture of f/4 at 200mm focal length, a horse, vehicle or other object is never completely in focus, but only between 9.7m and 10.3m. At 400mm focal length this figure is only reached at 20m distance.

In both cases and at the quoted distances, only an aperture of f/16 would provide a depth of field zone of 2.6m. A depth of field surrounding the subject can therefore only be created by using high-speed films, but even then only up to a certain reproduction scale. But first of all the photographer must be familiar with the camera and be sure that the subject won't be lost from the viewfinder in the meantime.

All focal length settings above 135mm are ideal for the sports program. But only lenses above 200mm focal length are generally considered super-telephoto lenses and are therefore specialities for sports photography.

Multiple Exposures

Film is a medium for storing light, in the same way that a tape stores magnetic impulses. Every decent tape recorder is capable of 'overplaying' or 'mixing'. It is not widely known that something comparable exists in photography. You need to abandon the idea that every picture is a document. If you consider the 150-year-old silver film purely as a medium for storing images and look at some video clips in amazement, you will soon feel like the sorcerer's apprentice who couldn't get rid of the spirits he had conjured up. In other words, once you've caught the bug for visual games, you'll never again be bored or lack subjects.

There's no better way to learn photographic technique, and especially to come to grips with the finer details of exposure, than by experimenting. Anyone who has mastered a five-fold multiple exposure in technical perfection (and not just as a happy accident), will understand much better many of the automatic solutions of their camera. But they will also know the camera's limitations, when they have to give a helping hand if a certain result is to be achieved. But let's get back to double and multiple exposures.

In the simplest form of multiple exposure, a piece of film is exposed not just with one subject but with two. If this takes place in front of a dark or even black background, any number of separate subject details can be accommodated on a piece of film without changing anything on the camera, other than the desired number of exposures. Every subject detail is exposed normally. 'Normally' in this case means in relation to the detail, and this is most easily achieved with partial metering, so that the background cannot influence the metering result.

The exposure setting must only be taken into account when any elements of the picture overlap. The film can only cope with one dose of the light intensity defined by its speed if it is to store a precise image of a subject.

As this light intensity is only geared to one exposure, a double exposure exposes overlapping details at twice the intensity. That's why every single exposure must be reduced so that, where details overlap, the sum of all exposures is equal to the figure for an ideal overall exposure.

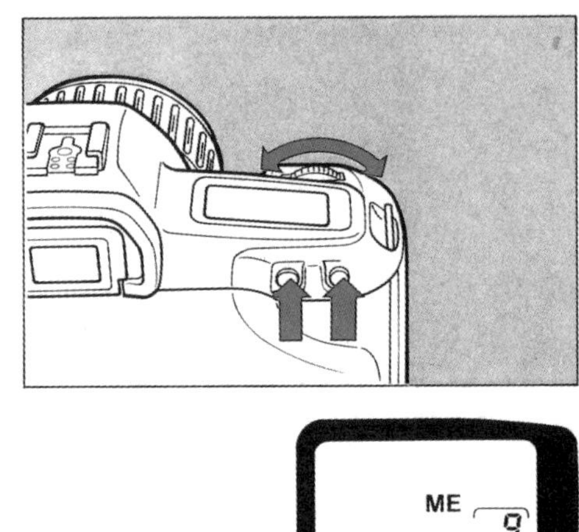

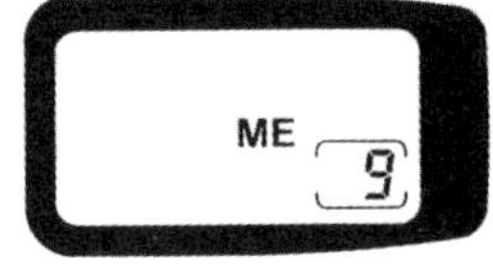

To make the calculation easier, the compensation values are input as exposure values. One exposure value less means that the aperture either has to be stopped down by one stop, or the shutter speed increased by one step. The same can be achieved with a negative compensation of 1 EV.

The most important question with multiple exposures isn't 'How many exposures?' but 'How often are the separate image details going to overlap?'. Many textbooks, and also the manual for the Canon EOS 1000, recommend that for two exposures a reduction of the exposure value by 1 is advisable. But this only applies to situations where the first and second exposures overlap in part or completely. In this case each shot should be underexposed by one stop or shutter speed step. For a three-fold exposure the exposure must obviously be compensated by the exposure value -1.5: each frame only gets one-third of the normal exposure. For a four-fold exposure the compensation factor is -2. But if the subjects only overlap twice, the compensation should be as for a double exposure.

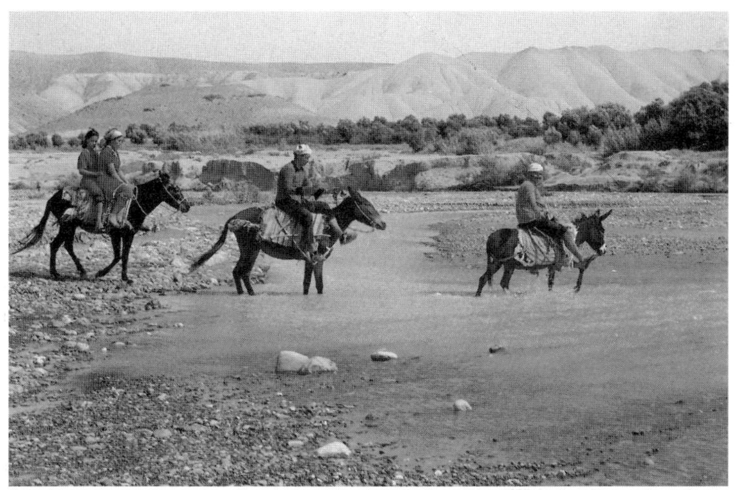
Scenes like this are best captured with a tele zoom, which allows an exact selection of the image section without a change in shooting position.

On the EOS 1000 the compensation factor is input simply by means of the exposure compensation button and the electronic input dial. Once the compensation factor has been set by turning the electronic input dial, it is displayed on the LCD panel. The factor itself is also shown in the viewfinder.

With the EOS 1000 you can even carry out nine-fold exposures. But while a compensation factor of -3.5 would be logical, in practice this is unrealistic, and the maximum compensation is -2. Positive compensation can also be carried out by the same factor, but not on multiple exposures. If parts of the subject only overlap twice or three times in a nine-fold exposure, only the necessary factor -1 or -1.5 must be input. A light background should always be counted as an additional overlap.

Multiple exposures can be carried out in all the creative programs, but none of the subject settings. But first you have to press both buttons on the back of the camera. At this point all symbols on the LCD panel disappear, and only the 'ME' symbol and a single number are visible. You can then set the desired number of exposures by turning the electronic input dial. As soon as the two buttons are released, part of the original display reappears.

The exception is the 'ME' indication which remains, and the number of frames remaining on the film, which is replaced by the number of exposures the current frame is to have.

Once all the multiple exposures have been carried out, the original data reappear in full in the viewfinder.

Controllable Automatic Exposure Programs

The other half of the command dial is intended for advanced photographers who already know the parameters which need to be mastered in order to achieve successful photographs. The operating modes of the EOS are shown on it in the now generally accepted way, as the initial letters of the English names for the automatic exposure programs:

P stands for the fully automatic program which, unlike the 'green zone' program, can be influenced by the photographer in several ways, or is subject to values pre-selected by the photographer.

Tv stands for 'Time value priority', generally known as shutter-priority. The photographer selects the shutter speed, and the aperture is determined by the camera accordingly.

Av is short for 'Aperture value priority', generally known as aperture-priority. The camera determines the shutter speed according to a preselected aperture.

dEP, displayed on the command dial, in the viewfinder and on the LCD panel, stands for 'depth of focus', the depth of field program. In this program the aperture is automatically determined by the camera's exposure control system, according to a depth of field specified by the photographer selecting the closest (dEP 1) and most distant (dEP 2) points for everything in between to be reproduced in focus.

M stands for manual mode.

The LCD panel shows the relevant operating data for the preselected program, and shutter speed and aperture data are visible in the viewfinder when the camera's electronic system is activated.

In all programs the exposure is normally determined either with the three-zone metering system, or by integral metering (on A-TTL or TTL flash control).

However, when photographing with the intelligent automatic program, aperture-priority, shutter-priority, or in manual mode it is always possible to switch to partial metering and AE focus lock which is shown as a star symbol in the viewfinder.

In manual mode the exposure is adjusted on the +/- scale.

Automatic program

In the automatic program the aperture and shutter speed for a correct exposure are automatically determined by the camera; if necessary, use of a flashgun is requested by a flashing [flash] symbol. The camera's exposure control system takes into account the focal length of the lens used, and the reciprocal of the focal length forms the start of the control curve for the shutter speed. On zoom lenses the course of the curve can be adjusted to the relevant value of 1/focal-length up to five times, depending on the selected focal length and different lens speeds.

From 30 seconds until the reciprocal is reached, the exposure at the widest aperture is controlled only by adjusting the shutter speed. As long as the selected shutter speed is slower than the reciprocal of the focal length, the camera gives a camera shake warning by flashing the symbol. This can also be regarded as a request to switch on the integral flash. If there is sufficient light for the shutter speed to exceed the 1/focal-length value, the actual automatic program starts to adjust shutter speed and aperture values together.

Some people may find it irritating if shutter speed and aperture values suddenly appear not just at the 'normal' numbers and if the viewfinder shows, for example, a aperture/shutter speed combination of f/13 and $^1/_{750}$ sec. The electromagnetically controlled iris diaphragm of the EOS lenses means that even values such as these can be set without any problems and with extreme precision. 'Odd' shutter speed values, such as $^1/_{900}$ sec, have been around for some time.

Photographers can easily adjust this fully automatic P-program to their own desires or needs at any time, for one shot at a time.

By means of the practical electronic input dial the shutter speed and aperture can be altered together, without taking the camera away from the eye. As the data is easily visible in the viewfinder, the adjustment achieved by turning the electronic input dial is immediately recognisable. This adjustment of the automatically selected shutter speed/aperture combination is called 'program shifting'.

All available aperture values and corresponding shutter speeds for a metered light situation can therefore be selected by turning the electronic input dial. A light situation corresponding to the light value 13, and a standard 50mm,f/1.8 lens would yield the following combinations (to be considered without intermediate values): f/2 and $^1/_{2000}$ sec, f/2.8 and $^1/_{1000}$ sec, f/4 and $^1/_{500}$ sec, f/5.6 and $^1/_{250}$ sec, f/8 and $^1/_{125}$ sec, and so on, down to f/22 and $^1/_{15}$ sec. So you can individually adjust the automatic program for fast shutter speeds on moving subjects, or vice versa for a particularly wide depth of field; and it is all done with one finger, which can return to the shutter button immediately afterwards - and you don't have to switch off the automatic program or take the camera away from the eye.

On zoom lenses program shift should only take place once the actual focal length to be used has been selected, otherwise the aperture values will change when the focal length is adjusted. Don't worry if you get a minimum aperture of f/22 on one occasion, and another time one of f/27, on the same lens! This means that you are using a zoom lens which has a different initial aperture for its shortest focal length than for its longest. (The speed of a lens is a relative value: focal length divided by the diameter of the maximum aperture.) So the lens will say, for example, 28-70mm,f/3.5-4.5, and the maximum aperture of f/3.5 will go with 28mm focal length, and f/4.5 with 70mm.

Shifting the shutter speed/aperture combination is only possible in the extended automatic program, and when the command dial is set to P. In the fully automatic program, when the command dial is set to green zone, these interventions are not possible.

Shutter-priority

By setting the command dial to Tv mode, the camera is switched to shutter-priority. This means that the photographer can pre-select a shutter speed between 30 and $^1/_{1000}$ sec in half-steps. The camera then automatically determines an aperture value suitable for the light conditions and the selected shutter speed. The camera always suggests a standard speed of 125 (for $^1/_{125}$ sec). If an aperture value is continuously lit in the viewfinder and on the LCD panel, the camera has selected the aperture determined by the multiple zone metering system. But if the maximum aperture value of the lens is flashing in one of the two indicators, then there is a danger of under-exposure. The shutter speed has to be reduced by means of the electronic input dial until the flashing stops and the aperture value indication is continuously lit.

If, on the other hand, the minimum aperture of the lens is flashing, then there is a danger of over-exposure. The shutter speed has to be reduced by turning the electronic input dial until the aperture value stops flashing. Partial metering can also be used in this program.

Shutter-priority is used mainly when the photographer needs a particular shutter speed for creative reasons. In this program the aperture is used exclusively to control the amount of light. Its creative effect is disregarded in favour of the necessary shutter speed. Fast shutter speeds up to $^1/_{1000}$ sec are preselected, for example, for photographing from a vehicle, when using a large reproduction ratio, for sports shots of fast movements, or for fast-moving subjects. Fast shutter speeds generally serve to freeze movement. But it also works the other way around: slow shutter speeds in combination with shutter-priority mode can be used creatively to achieve wipe effects, for example of a motorcycle race.

Using the Tv program with preselected shutter speeds of one or more seconds makes sense even for architectural shots. In this

---

Shots of structures and patterns frequently found in nature appear more three-dimensional in side or streaking light.

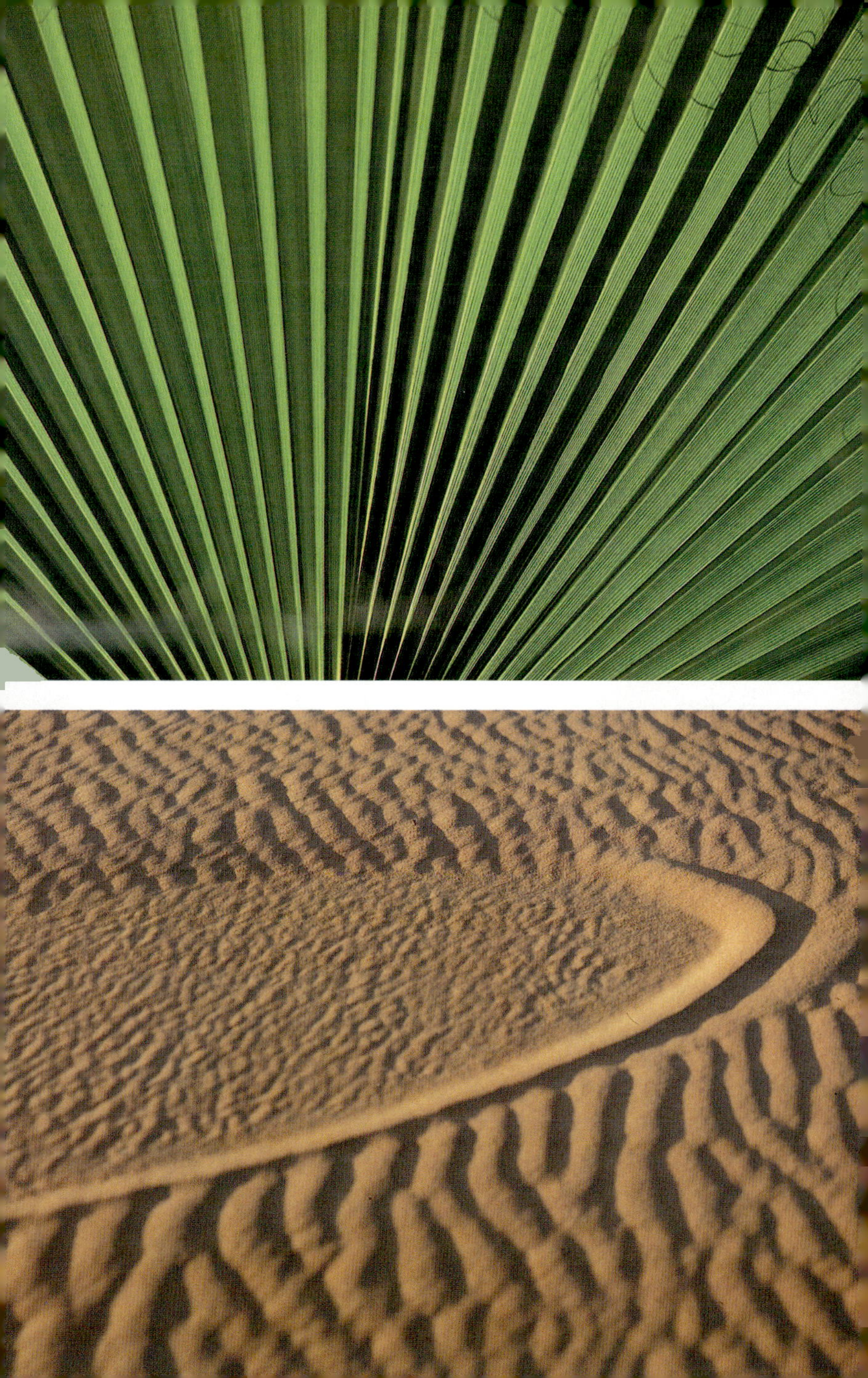

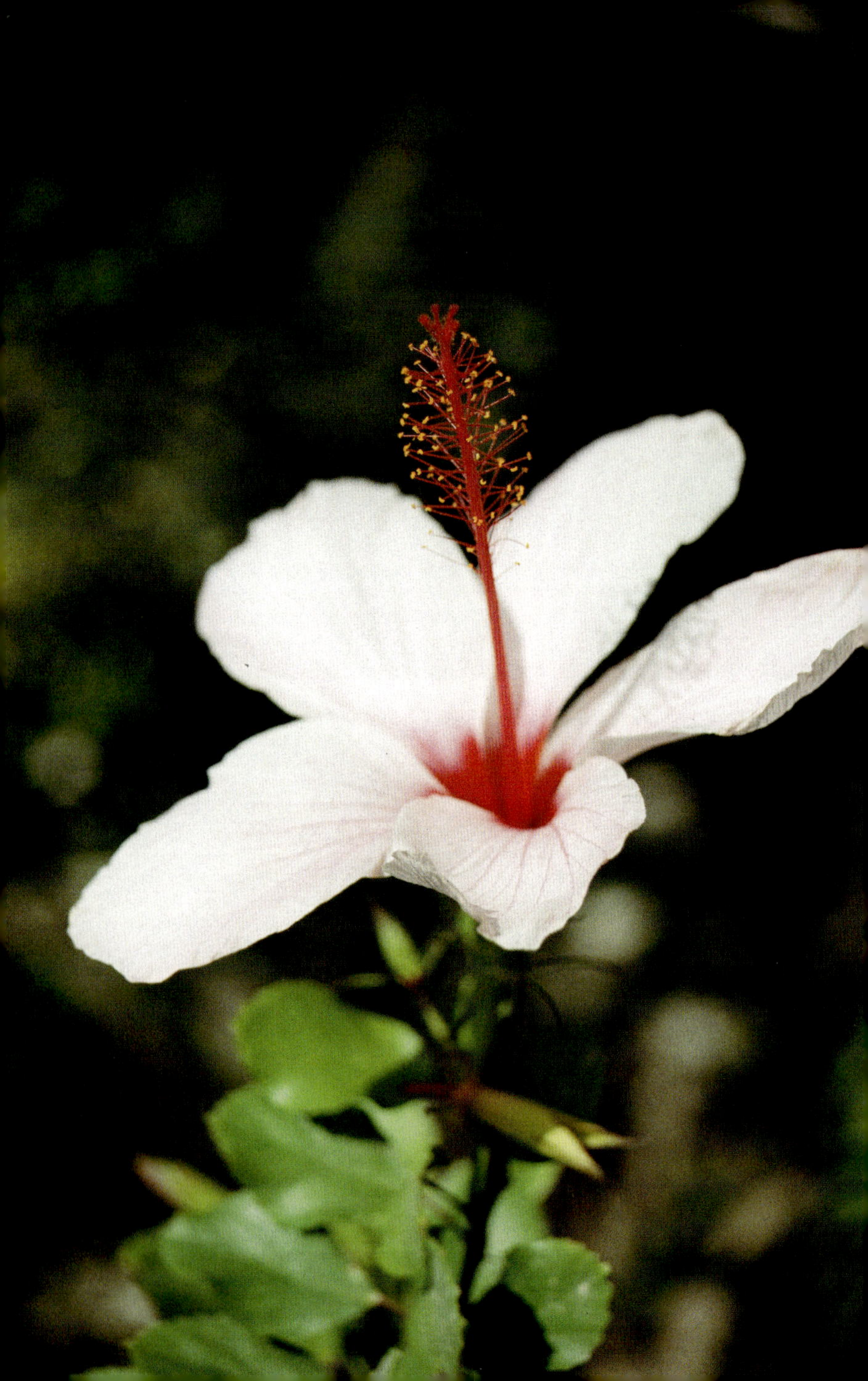

case everything which moves during exposure - cars or people - is reproduced as a blur.

On very long exposures the subjects moving across the shot become completely invisible. This is a popular trick, for example, to make a busy square appear deserted.

Aperture-priority

In aperture-priority the photographer selects the aperture. The standard value suggested by the camera is always f/5.6. The exposure control system automatically determines the necessary shutter speed, taking into account the available brightness distribution of the light.

Up to now this exposure mode has been the right program when the spatial impression is to determine the image effect of the subject; that is, whenever the depth of field is important. On the one hand, a small depth of field could be desirable - for example to make the most of the face in a portrait shot whilst the background disappears in unsharpness. On the other hand, it could be necessary for the sharpness to reach from the foreground all the way into the background, particularly to achieve effective landscape or architectural shots. But for the EOS 1000 these are subjects which are mastered better, more easily, and far more precisely with the depth of field program.

In the aperture-priority program the threat of wrong exposure is also indicated by flashing: underexposure only when a shutter speed of 30 sec is still too slow, overexposure when even $^1/_{1000}$ sec is too fast. In both cases the aperture is adjusted by turning the electronic input dial.

In aperture-priority mode the exposure can be determined both by multiple zone and partial metering.

The depth of field is reduced noticeably at large reproduction ratios. Often only a few millimetres are available. The close-up program automatically selects the optimum aperture depending on the light conditions.

Automatic depth of field

Photographic subjects mostly have a three-dimensional character. Lenses, however, project only one single plane, the focusing plane, onto the film.

Only that which is on this single plane is reproduced sharply - as a dot. Any subject located in front of, or behind, this plane, can no longer be reproduced as dots; this is where unsharp areas of varying sizes are formed, the so-called circles of confusion.

The human eye does not see as sharply as the lens, and deviations from dot-shaped reproduction therefore only become noticeable on close inspection. Everything below a certain size is not perceived at all. This is why there is an area in front of, and even more so behind, the focal plane, which still appears sharp to the human eye, although in physical terms it isn't. This seemingly spatial extension is known as depth of field.

Every single circle of confusion is influenced by the aperture. As the aperture becomes wider, the circle of confusion becomes larger, and the depth of field area is reduced. This effect also works the other way around: as the aperture is narrowed, the circles of confusion become smaller; they therefore appear sharper, and the depth of field in front of, and behind, the focusing plane increases. As this is more noticeable at small reproduction ratios than at large ones, it is often wrongly assumed that wide-angle lenses - which reproduce more of the subject and therefore show everything smaller - have a wider depth of field than telephoto lenses. But enlargements of an identical image section, shot with a telephoto and a wide-angle lens, clearly show an identical depth of field. However, it depends on the quality of the lens whether the transition from sharpness to unsharpness remains clean and flowing, or whether it is full of colour seams. The sharp point is mostly correct only for one colour of the visible spectrum. You should judge your EOS lenses particularly for this quality - even as zoom lenses they show amazingly high reproduction performance.

The depth of field can also be calculated mathematically and is shown in depth of field tables available for every focal length.

To save you the need to study long tables, the EOS 1000 has a 'DEP' program. This offers the photographer a simple, or a very precise way of determining the area to be reproduced sharply in the shot.

What is estimated in the shutter-priority program, or selected according to tables, can here be determined or metered. Once the points limiting the desired depth of field have been chosen, the camera selects the necessary aperture. The photographer first points at the start and end points of the desired depth of field. When the shutter button is pressed halfway, a signal in the viewfinder indicates that the metering process has taken place. The camera then calculates the aperture required to achieve the desired result, taking into account the pre-determined values and the lens used. Canon's literature tells us that the camera focuses on the value between the two metered distances, but this is not in fact accurate. In reality the metered distance is divided into 17 partial distances. The first seven ensure depth of field in front of, the remaining ten the spatial extension behind the focusing plane, which is therefore located exactly between the seventh and eight partial distance. This 7:10 ratio is very practice-orientated, and the stronger increase in the depth of field towards the back is easily explained. That which is in front of the focusing plane is closer to the camera and therefore recorded at a larger reproduction ratio than what lies behind it, which is recorded at smaller ratio and is therefore surrounded by a smaller circle of confusion.

But let's return to photographic practice: the camera is set to the 'DEP' program, the focus mark pointed at the nearest point and the shutter button pressed halfway. 'dEP 1' and the focus symbol appear in the viewfinder. Pressure on the shutter button is then released, the camera pointed at the far point for the desired depth of field, and the shutter button is once more pressed halfway until 'dEP 2' and the focus signal appear in the viewfinder. When you press the shutter button halfway for the third time, the aperture necessary for the selected depth of field, and the shutter speed resulting from it, will appear in the viewfinder and on the LCD panel. At the same time both values are fed into the camera electronics.

If the aperture is insufficient to ensure a sharp reproduction of the desired area, the smallest aperture number of the lens will flash. If you still press the shutter button all the way down, you will get a correct exposure according to the results of multiple zone metering, with the smallest possible aperture.

But if there is sufficient time to focus once again, you should reduce the required depth of field or the reproduction ratio.

To do this, you can step back from the subject, or use a shorter focal length from the same shooting position, and start again by metering the closest point.

If the minimum aperture already mentioned is flashing, you will at least get a correctly exposed shot; if minimum aperture and shutter speed are both flashing in the viewfinder you will get an incorrect exposure. You cannot use a flash when there is too little light - the automatic depth of field program does not work with flash.

When using zoom lenses, the focal length must not be changed once the closest point has been selected; if it is, the whole process has to be abandoned and repeated. This means waiting until the indicator light goes out, after approx 10 sec. You can also switch the 'DEP' program off and on again by means of the command dial.

If the same distance is metered twice, the camera automatically reduces the depth of field to the minimum.

The automatic depth of field program is certainly one of the most important creative tools for everybody who wants to take creative shots and has very precise ideas about photographic results. You can practise making optimum use of this program. To do this, you should take as many shots as possible with a tripod. It is advisable to proceed systematically: first take a shot with a relatively narrow, then one with maximum depth of field. When evaluating their shots many people will realise that they initially overestimated the necessary depth of field whilst substantially underestimating the aperture and shutter speed.

Many subject areas and tasks previously solved with aperture- or shutter-priority can now be mastered far more precisely with the automatic depth of field program. Speedway races are a good example. The EOS 1000 can be set to the sports program, which is pre-programmed for fast shutter speed with an initial aperture of f/5.6 and AI servo autofocus. When the motorcyclist appears in the viewfinder, the shutter button is pressed early, and the pre-calculating autofocus functions perfectly. The camera automatically switches to continuous exposure. But it is more than doubtful whether you will get a super shot rather than just high film consumption. Why not set the camera to 'DEP' mode and pre-program a distance, for example from the centre of a bend to its end, or to a big muddy puddle? Or you could point at the top of a hump the motorcyclist will jump over (dEP 2) and the area of ground he will land on (dEP 1). In this way you can pre-focus a photographic highlight in each case, and you simply wait until one or more motorbikes appear and press the shutter button at the right moment. You are guaranteed to get a sharp shot, and you're saving film.

The depth of field calculation is based on a circle of confusion of $^1/_{30}$mm in diameter, which will appear as a sharp point in prints up to 13/18cm as far as the eye is concerned. If you are looking for greater enlargement factors you should stop down the aperture by at least one stop by shifting with the electronic input dial.

Whilst the EOS 1000 automatically masters an extremely high number of photographic situations, the photographer still has to apply and utilise its technology in a meaningful way in order to achieve really outstanding pictures. You should plan your shots and the best use of the camera's technology precisely in order to be able to calculate the effects exactly.

Manual exposure control

In this mode both aperture and shutter speed are selected manually. When set to 'manual', the camera displays a standard setting of $^1/_{125}$ sec and f/5.6. Exposure adjustment to determine the necessary shutter speed/aperture combination is carried out by means of the electronic input dial. The shutter speed is adjusted directly. To select the aperture the exposure compensation button on the left of the back of the camera needs to be pressed as well.

By always sticking to the same sequence you can carry out manual metering surprisingly fast. You turn the electronic input dial until the desired shutter speed appears.

You can then see the shutter speed and aperture in the viewfinder. The metering system takes the pre-selected shutter speed as the basis for metering. The exposure compensation scale in the viewfinder and on the LCD panel shows the deviation from the correct exposure in half-stops between +/-2 light values. If the deviation exceeds two aperture stops in either direction, the indicator will be above one of the two triangles at the extremes of the scale. To set the correct exposure, the indicator has to be aligned with the centre mark by adjusting either the shutter speed or the aperture value.

Manual metering is carried out as multiple zone or partial metering. If you want to meter with pinpoint precision, for example, partial metering in connection with zoom lenses should always be carried out in the telephoto setting. But partial metering only makes sense if you really do meter the correct points, otherwise the danger of incorrect exposure is far higher than with multiple zone metering. In critical cases a grey card provides an optimum metering area. All exposure meters, including that of the Canon EOS 1000, are standardised to the 18% reflectivity of a grey card, at least for partial metering.

You can often see from sports programs on television that the brightness of the image changes when the camera switches from wide-angle to super-telephoto setting. It becomes lighter if details are in the shade, or darker in full light. The same can happen in photography, because you will normally have to cope with bigger differences in brightness in the wide-angle range than on detail shots with the telephoto lens. This fact can easily be observed by changing the focal length of a zoom lens, where you will notice differences in metering between the shortest and longest focal length, even if a correct exposure is made in both cases. Such fluctuations can be avoided by using the partial metering method. It is suitable for all critical light situations which are too much even for multiple zone metering, as soon as you are looking for creative solutions, not just technically perfect ones. Only the photographer knows which image detail is to receive optimum light, even the most sophisticated automatic exposure system won't be able to calculate that.

The photographer himself must decide what is to receive optimum light, particularly in situations where there are extreme differences in brightness between the main subject and the background; this could happen, for example, on stage shots or backlit subjects which, as has already been mentioned, don't just have to be exposed correctly, but in a way to suit the photographic idea. A portrait of a girl in front of a sunset, for example, or a backlit mill can be realised with six different exposures without any difficulty. All the results will be usable, but their moods will differ markedly.

If the sun is used as the point for partial metering in these examples, you will get a silhouette with an almost nocturnal character. The exact opposite will happen when the darkest image sections are metered. The light sections of the shot will appear over bright, but otherwise the shot will have more of a soft, romantic mood. Everything between these two extremes will deliver pictures whose moods will also be in between those of the others. As partial metering has to be used purposefully, such shots can't be compared directly with exposure sequences of the same situations taken in the AEB (automatic exposure bracketing) function.

Long exposures

The automatically and manually controlled shutter speeds of the Canon EOS 1000 range from $^1/_{1000}$ second to 30 seconds. This range can be extended even further in manual exposure control mode. To do this, the Canon EOS in 'M' mode is set to 'bulb' - the next indication after '30' on the LCD panel - by means of the electronic input dial. The shutter stays open as long as the shutter button remains pressed. A tripod is an absolute necessity for such shots. It is probably obvious that the incorrect exposure warning of the Canon EOS 1000 is omitted in this manual setting, which exceeds the metering range.

Picture Composition with the EOS 1000

The EOS 1000 can deliver perfect exposures, but it is still the photographer's task to choose the subject and to determine what is to be in the frame. This is perhaps the prime creative opportunity, the most important and satisfying task, if photography is your hobby and if you don't just consider taking pictures as a means to visualise memories.

But first you have to learn to see, to look, in order to select the visually interesting aspects of the world you see around you. While our eye sees objects as images at an angle of vision of about 46°, it only sees clearly a much smaller angle. In addition, sharpness is concentrated on the area of greatest interest, so we have to start from a selective perception. And this selective perception is also the be-all and end-all of photography. The frame should only show what is important for the mood of the picture or its message. This is most easily achieved by leaving out everything that is superfluous - for example by getting very close to the subject, or by choosing a lens with a focal length which shows the subject filling the frame. This is why you should always set your zoom lens at the longest focal length in order to get the largest possible image when you first look through the camera. The picture content captured by the lens depends on the selected image section - which hopefully fills the frame.

A lens with a focal length of 50mm - or a zoom set at 50mm - sees approximately at the same angle of view as the human eye.

Shots taken at this focal length are always perceived as normal for this very reason. If the focal length is shorter - between about 40mm and 28mm - every millimetre less adds more of the subject to the shot. The angle of view of the lens widens in proportion to the decreasing focal length. If the angle of view becomes even wider by further shortening the focal length, we are in the extreme wide-angle area.

It goes in the opposite direction when you change the focal

length of your lens the other way, again starting from 50mm. The angle of view becomes smaller, a smaller image section is shown noticeably larger. Shots taken in the focal length range between 50mm and 100mm are still perceived as fairly normal, because they only offer the viewer a concentrated section of the image. The normal telephoto range lies between 100mm and 200mm, and this is where the binocular effect starts. Lenses with a focal length above 300mm are generally considered extreme telephoto lenses. But let's return to picture composition.

The main subject should always be clearly emphasised. When choosing the image section you should also take into account the picture composition.

As I have already said several times, the simplest way is for the subject to fill the entire frame.

If this is not possible because more of the subject is to be in the shot, light can give quality to the photograph.

The easiest way of emphasising the main subject is by lighting. A single spotlight aimed at a person draws the viewer's attention to this point. Nature offers similar effects which the photographer can use for the same purpose; a ray of light falling through a cloud can light a forest or a narrow street like a spotlight. Similar results are achieved with light/dark contrasts over a larger area, as for example the view through a window or a gateway. These are all mood subjects which used to cause the photographer problems, but which can now be captured without difficulty, thanks to the evaluative metering method of the EOS.

Colours also influence picture composition. Colour contrast creates visible differences; a person dressed in red standing in a green field will be immediately striking. Our eye perceives certain colours, for example shades of yellow, as particularly bright, whereas darker colours, such as blue and purple, are considerably less noticeable. Generally speaking, warm colours push themselves forward in photographs, whereas cold ones retreat into the background. This applies particularly to blue. This fact is often not taken into account sufficiently, especially with small subjects and still-life compositions. Also, light objects are more striking than dark ones, so every viewer will notice light spots in the background of a photograph.

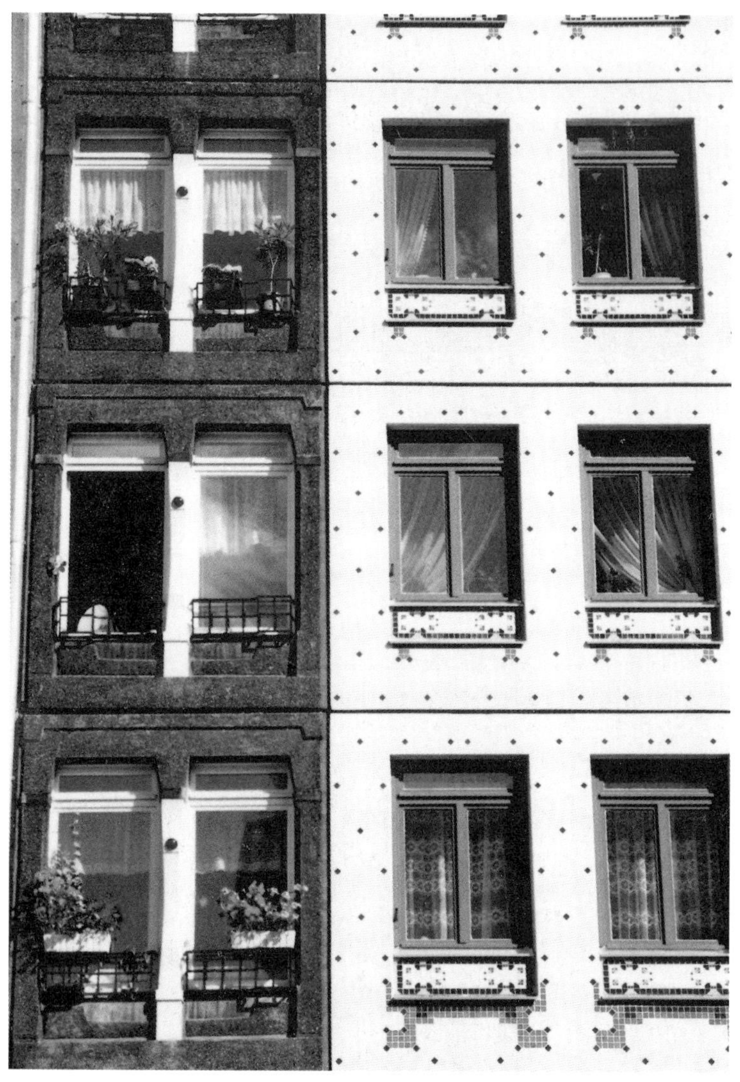

Graphic subjects are often particularly appealing if the shot was composed with a view to asymmetrical image division.

The three-zone metering system of the EOS 1000 delivers optimum exposure even with backlighting.

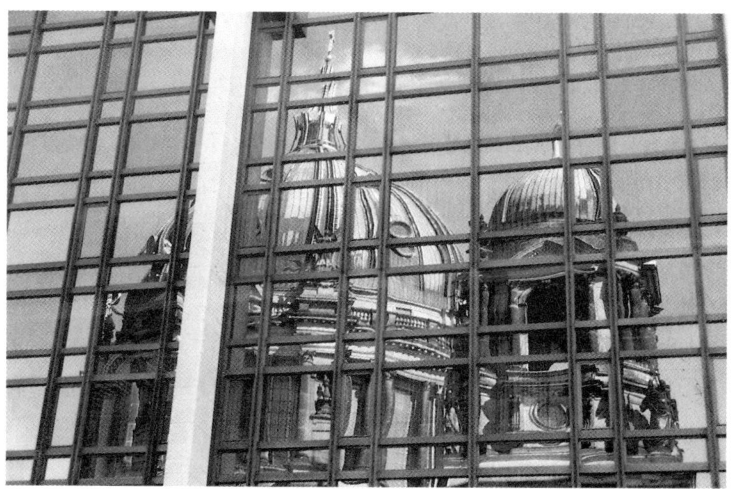

Reflections of impressive old buildings in a modern glass facade are always attractive.

Similarly, a sharp image is more likely to be noticed than one which isn't sharp. This is why experimenting with selective focus can be particularly impressive. A sharp detail in the foreground, in front of an unsharp background, is always appealing. A portrait with an unsharp background allows the eye to rest on the subject. Selective focus is therefore one of the big secrets of good photography. And the DEP program of the EOS 1000 can be used for this purpose to great effect. The DEP program can determine even minimal depth of field zones, and is therefore one of the most important programs from a purely creative point of view.

The Graphic Shape

A picture composition which can be read and understood by the viewer creates interest in the photograph. This is more easily achieved through a graphic picture composition.

If you ever get the chance to look at the thousands of photographs produced by a big laboratory in one day, many of them will give you a strange impression; they look as if the photographer had just discovered the subject and had taken the photograph in this exact situation, at the distance he or she just happened to be from the subject. But it is not the best possible photograph of the subject. Something interesting has been presented in a photographically unsuitable way, because the photographer has failed to take into account a number of points. Firstly, the way the camera sees differently from the eye. Our eye registers selectively. If it is interested in a subject - because of an optical signal, shape or colour - it only perceives this one subject.

The surrounding area - what is to the right and left of the object of interest, in front of it and behind - is not perceived voluntarily. This is why we get photographs of trees growing from people's heads, and many shots with the main subject far too tiny, even though nothing else of any interest is in the picture apart from it.

The EOS 1000 and its AF can cope even with poorly-lit subjects in museums.

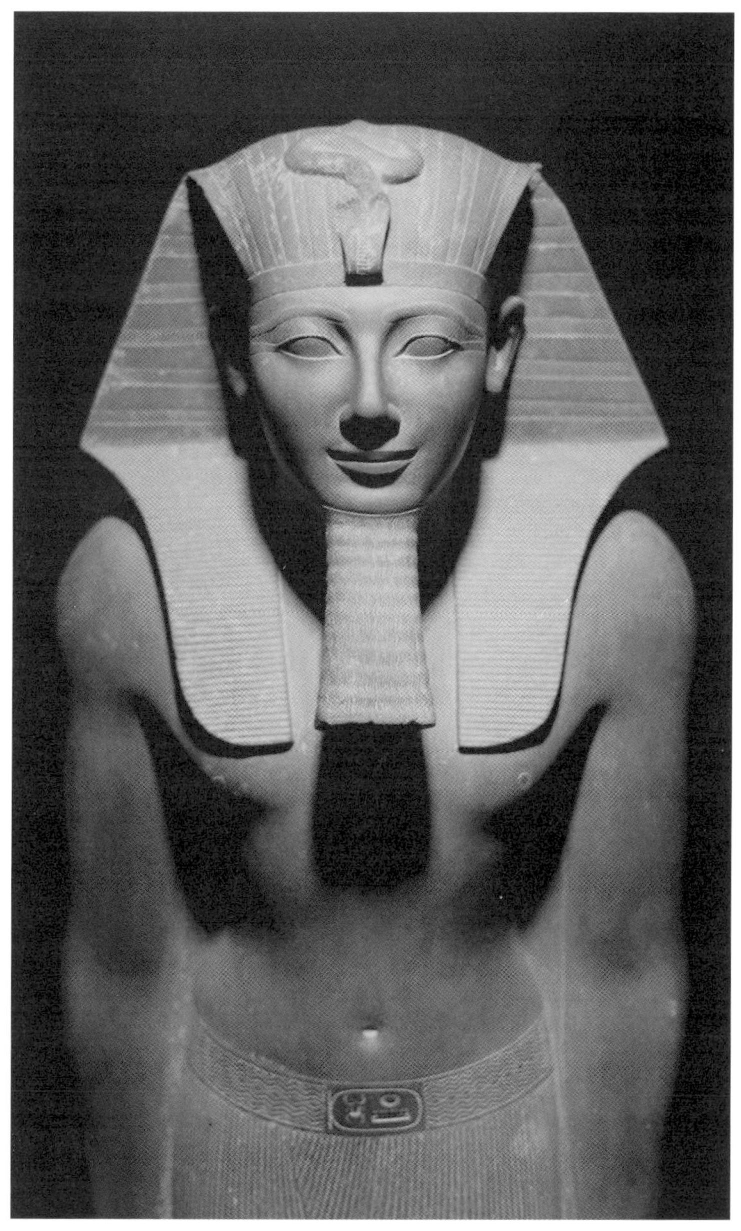

The camera simply registers. It registers everything it is offered, and it tries without fail to capture everything that is within its angle of view. The bright viewfinder image supports the photographer's selective way of seeing, because the focus area shows only that part of the subject which is in focus. The overall effect of the surrounding area is not normally shown. The viewfinder shows how the image would look with the widest aperture, and not how it will look for example in its distribution of light and dark areas. Mistakes in picture composition are therefore only noticed when it is too late and when the result is already in front of you. But the differences between our way of seeing and photographic reproduction are even bigger. If you discover a subject with a clear geometric shape, for example a door or a shop window, while you're standing at an angle to it, you will know that the door and the window consist of vertical and horizontal lines. Where these lines meet, they create an angle of $90°$. In nine out of ten cases you will not be able to measure a $90°$ angle on the finished photograph. You will find that either the vertical or the horizontal lines don't run parallel to the edge of the picture. The graphic and geometric image of the door in our mind's eye has therefore not been translated successfully into a photograph.

The camera only registers optical signals. It is therefore wrong to try and take photographs in the way the human eye sees the subject. You're guaranteed to be more successful the other way round, by looking at the subject in the way the lens sees it. If you can do this and draw the consequences from it, you will get more successful and presentable shots. The photographs must just become simpler. If everything superfluous is left out, the subject will become larger and have more detail, it will be clearer and more informative, more direct and more easily accessible, and therefore a lot better. That which appears larger in the photograph, which has a larger reproduction scale, shows more detail. Where there are more details in shape or colour, the message of the picture becomes clearer, and more information can be deduced from the photograph. Less subject also means that the picture composition is more accessible to the viewer.

To return to the example of the door; a graphically effective photograph of a door is taken in the portrait format, with the door frame running parallel to the edges of the picture. In many cases this means taking a few more steps to the side, to be immediately in front of the subject. So that the subject plane is parallel to the film plane. It couldn't be simpler.

It Depends On The Viewpoint

Its different lenses turn the EOS 1000 into a versatile tool, ideal for translating the photographer's ideas into pictures. With the EOS 1000 you must decide whether you want to use your own camera technique and select one of the creative programs, or whether you want to take the shot at one of the automatic subject settings.

The creative achievement is finding the subject, getting into position, and choosing which section of the image to use and when to take the photograph.

Different lenses can be useful here; they enable you to record the desired section of the image, which is then projected onto the film at a certain reproduction scale, from a chosen shooting distance. For example, if you change the focal length, either with a zoom lens or by changing lenses, without changing the shooting distance, the reproduction scale changes in relation to the new focal length. If the new focal length is shorter, the subject will be shown smaller and the subject area is larger. More is shown in the shot, inversely proportionate to the focal length. At a focal length of 35mm, everything is half the size of a 70mm setting; the reproduction scale doubles at 140mm. The ratio between 35mm and 140mm is 1:4.

An object which is two millimetres high in the first shot will be four times as high, eight millimetres, at 140mm. If the shooting distance is not changed, increasing focal length produces an increasing reproduction scale and an increasingly small part of the original subject appears in the shot. That's all! There's no change in perspective, but always a change in the reproduction scale. This is important if you want to take frame-filling shots. A knowledge of these changes in size can also help avoid mistakes in planning what lenses to buy, and it helps photographers with little knowledge about different lenses in judging the effective-

Effect of Focal Length

35mm

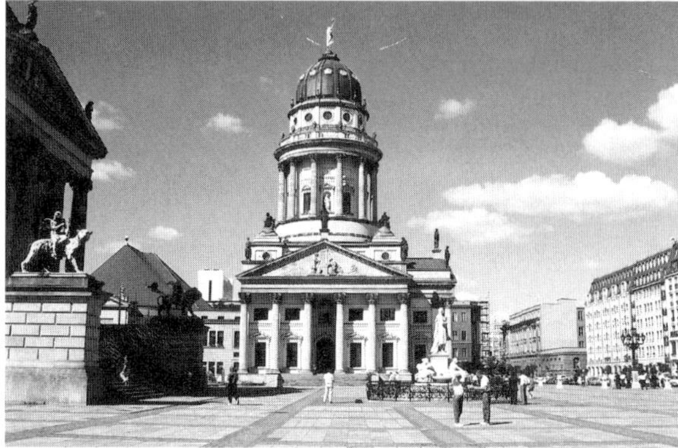

50mm

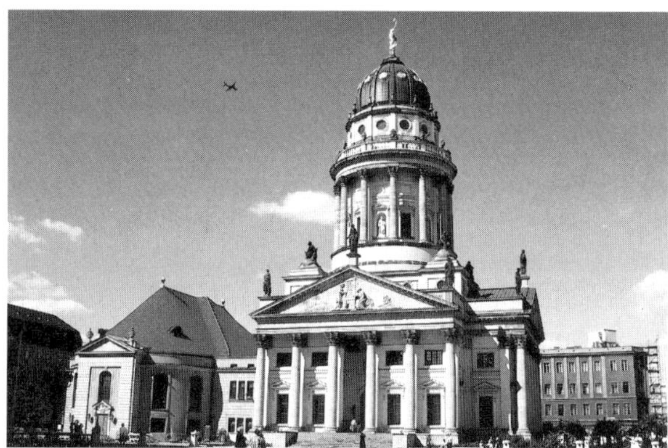

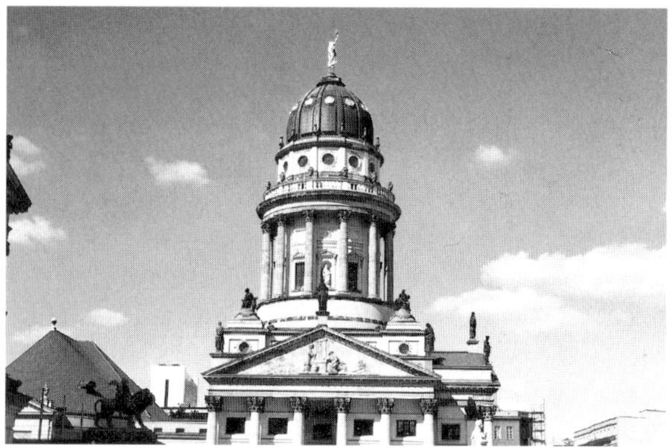

80mm

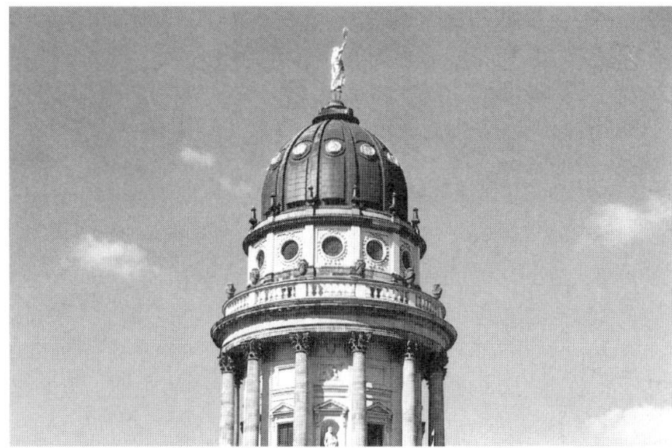

105mm

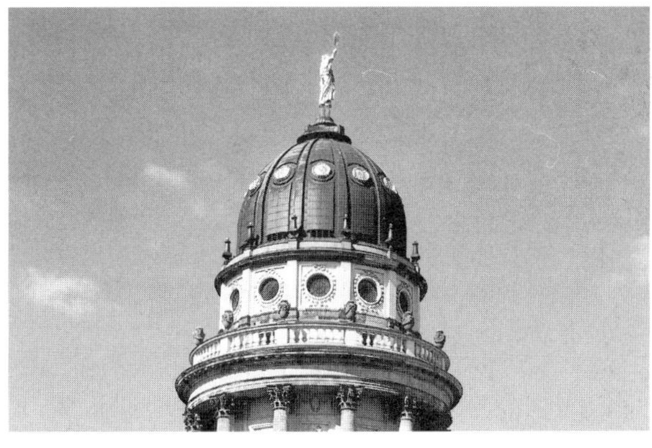

135mm

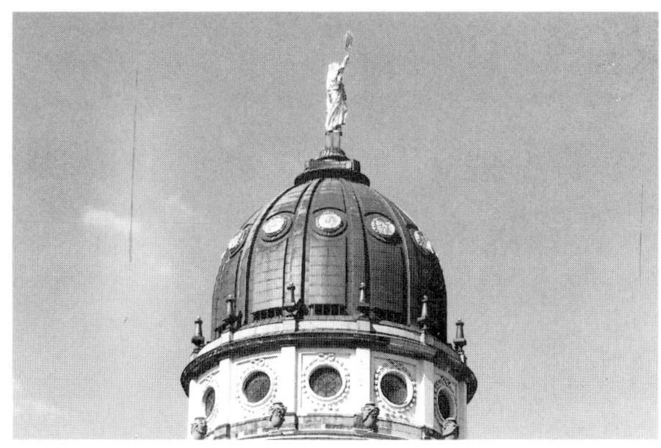

200mm

ness of zoom lenses. The reproduction scale doubles with a 35-70mm zoom lens; at 35-135mm the factor is almost 4, the same as a 50-200mm lens.

Focal Lengths

Whether you change lenses or change the focal length of a zoom lens, the perspective remains the same for all shots of a subject - if the shooting distance stays the same. You can only influence the perspective by changing the relationship between your main subject and the background by changing your position as well. But as there is much talk about dynamic wide-angle and space-condensing telephoto perspective, here are a few remarks about perspective and distortion.

The lines of a skyscraper photographed with the camera held at an angle are called converging verticals and are therefore a distortion. The lines of a railway track meeting in the distance are accepted as normal, even though both examples originated in the same laws of linear perspective. To create lifelike images according to the laws of linear perspective, artists used to employ the camera obscura, which projected an image of the scene onto a screen or table.

The undistorted reproduction of a subject is only possible in photography if the subject is two-dimensional. With three-dimensional subjects a flat surface must face the camera. In both cases the area to be reproduced must be exactly parallel to the focal plane, otherwise trapezium-shaped distortion occurs. Naturally this also applies to a circle. Reproduced in perspective it becomes an ellipse. Its circular shape remains only if its area is parallel to the focal plane. If it is not parallel, every subject is distorted.

Every reduction, fore-shortening or convergence (the meeting of parallels) is distortion in terms of perspective, but the visual experience of the photographer or the viewer differs. That which appears natural is in perspective, that which doesn't seem normal is distorted.

Through your choice of focal length and shooting distance you can determine the amount of distortion. Whether this distortion is accepted as normal perspective, as distortion, or even as a mistake depends on your photographic ability. The amount of distortion can be controlled precisely through the focal length of the lens and the viewpoint. It is therefore consciously employed in picture composition by creative photographers in order to intensify the information contained in a photograph, or to increase its emotional message.

If you want to take as many different shots as possible of one subject, this is achieved most easily by changing the focal length and shooting distance. Halving the shooting distance and focal length delivers shots with a steep perspective. The foreground is emphasised in size, the vanishing lines appear to converge more quickly in the background. The effect is reversed if both subject distance and focal length are doubled; foreground and background appear to have moved closer together while the image section remains the same.

This effect is, of course, achieved easily with a zoom lens, but only if you change the shooting distance at the same time.

In comparable situations photographers frequently use a lens which is seemingly dictated by circumstances. For example, many photographers automatically reach for a wide-angle lens when they want to take a shot of a narrow lane full of bustling life. The result is usually boring, because the wide-angle lens changes the relationship between foreground and background in such a way that the near foreground is reproduced relatively large and the background extremely small. In a shot taken with a focal length of 24mm, a stallholder standing less than two metres away will appear as far away as if his stall was at the end of a wide lane. This is suggested by the large foreground and the change in size in relation to the background. In this situation the photographer who wants to convey the feeling and atmosphere of an overflowing lane will go back further and use a telephoto lens. The space-condensing effect, the recognisable linear perspective, suddenly fills the same lane with a milling crowd. Every lens therefore has its typical seeing habits, which are very much influenced by the relationship between the shooting distance and the subject, and that between the subject and the background.

The Canon EF Lens System

Canon is one of the few camera manufacturers who have from the beginning placed great importance on offering their own comprehensive lens system. It is therefore not surprising that pioneering work in lens design is often associated with the Canon name. This is epitomised in the motors which drive the autofocus lenses. Canon have developed two different types of focusing motor to build into the EF lenses; one is a small electronic motor transferring power by means of a mechanical coupling to the movable optical elements and its whirring noise is quite distinctive. The other is an almost silent ultrasonic motor which drives a diaphragm movements are transferred to the focusing lens elements by ultrasonic waves.

Aspherical elements, internal focusing, and floating elements all indicate the pinnacle of lens technology. Each technique is suited to a particular type of lens and where appropriate, Canon apply it.

Canon's emphasis on image quality is also witnessed by the fact that all lenses have the same colour quality thanks to these improvements, and that an ingenious design feature offers maximum protection against reflections within the lens.

The full range of Canon EF lenses is shown in the table below. Many are unlikely to be of interest to EOS 1000 users because they are designed for special purposes or to give the highest level of optical performance in very demanding professional work, but they are described in the next chapter all the same. However, you many well want to round off your EOS 1000 outfit by adding one or two fixed focus lenses - perhaps a 24mm or 28mm wide-angle

Old doors are popular subjects for people who like to collect pictures on a theme. A tele zoom and the sports program are right for snapshots and action shots as those shown at the top of the following pages. The landscape and depth of field program are equally suitable for rows of houses as those in Morocco shown at the bottom of page 88. The close-up program is advisable for structures as those shown at the bottom of page 89.

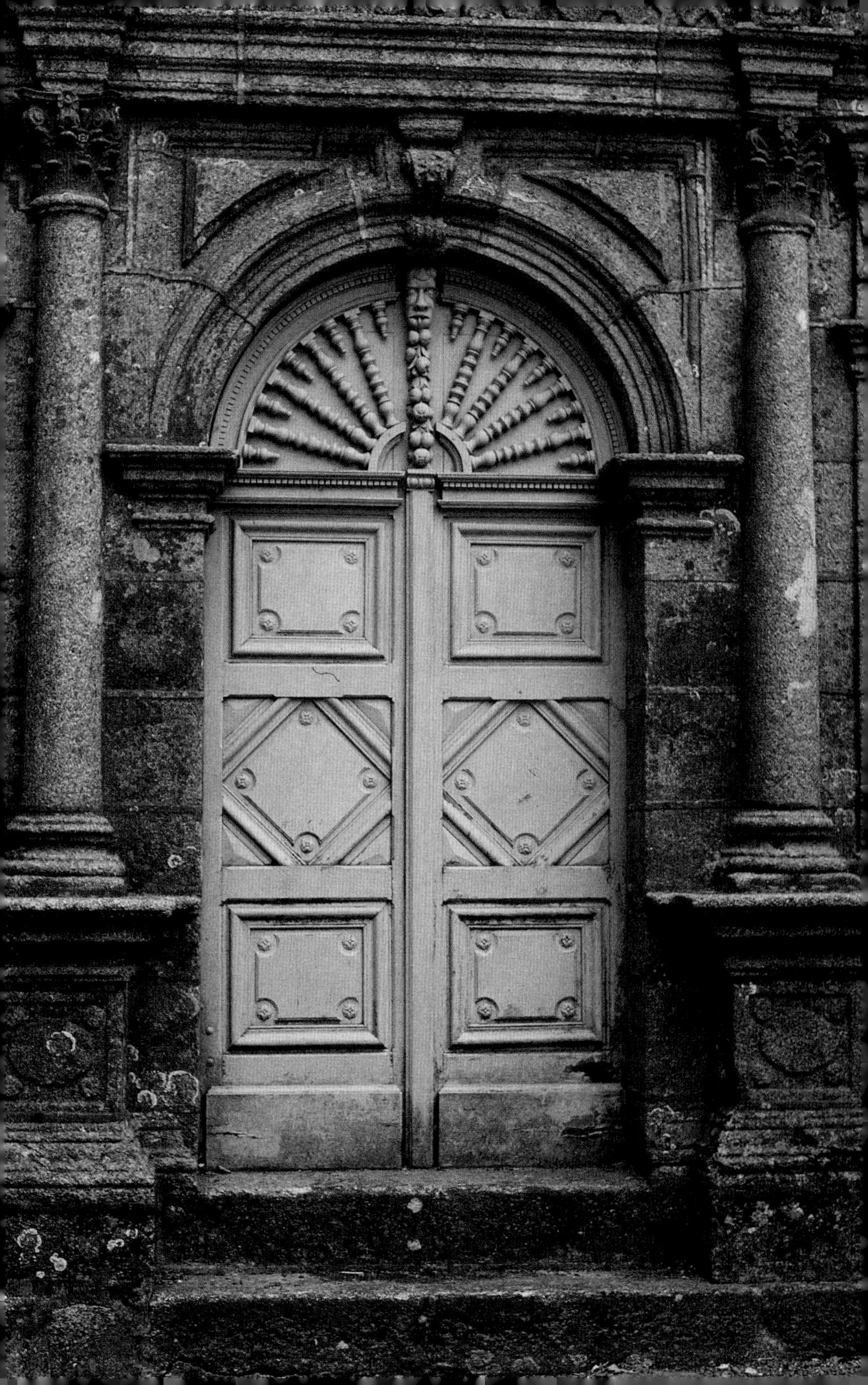

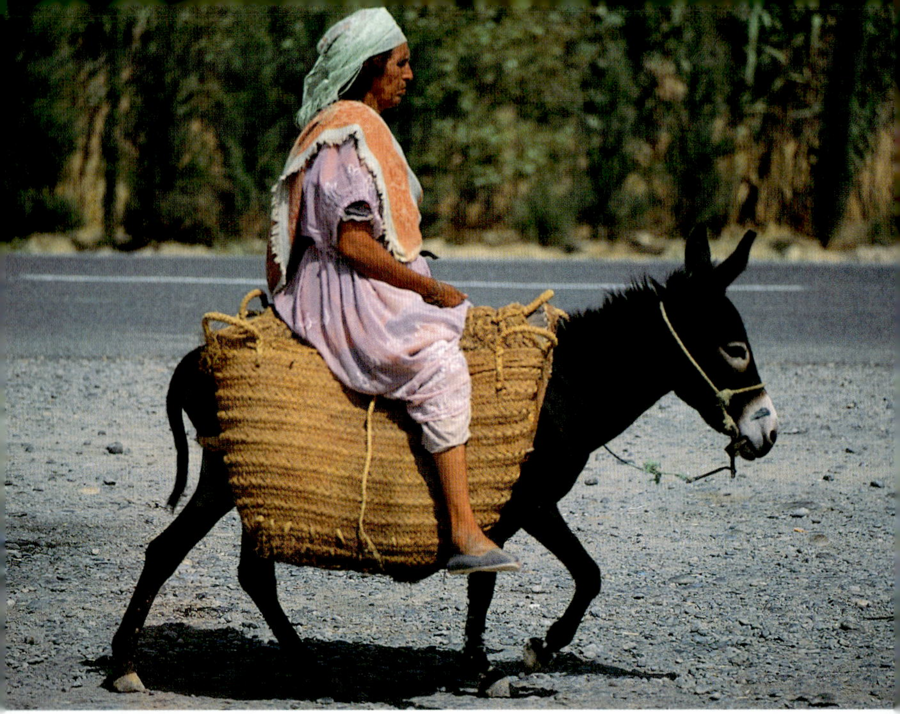

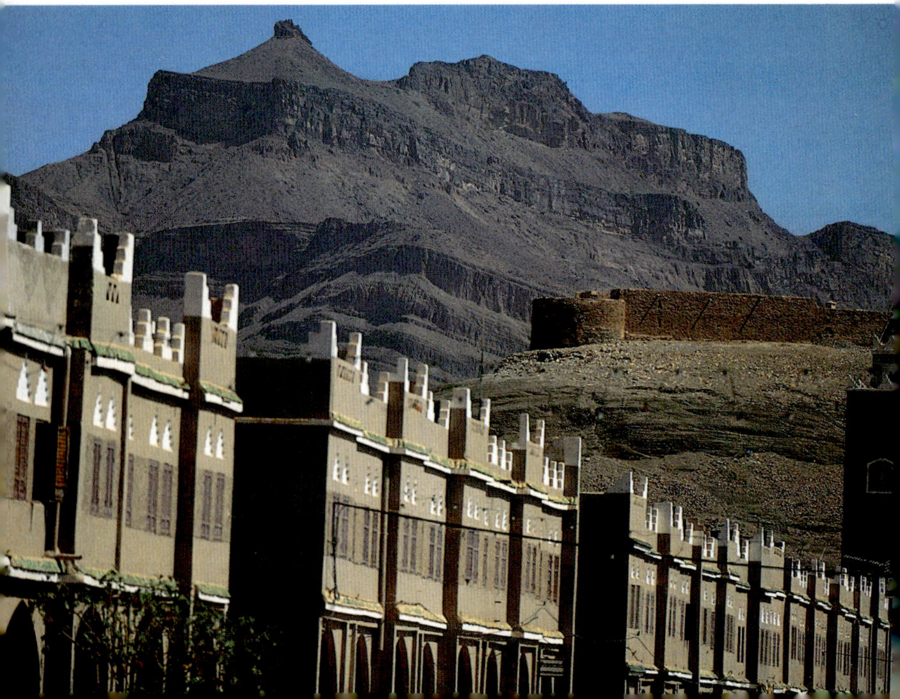

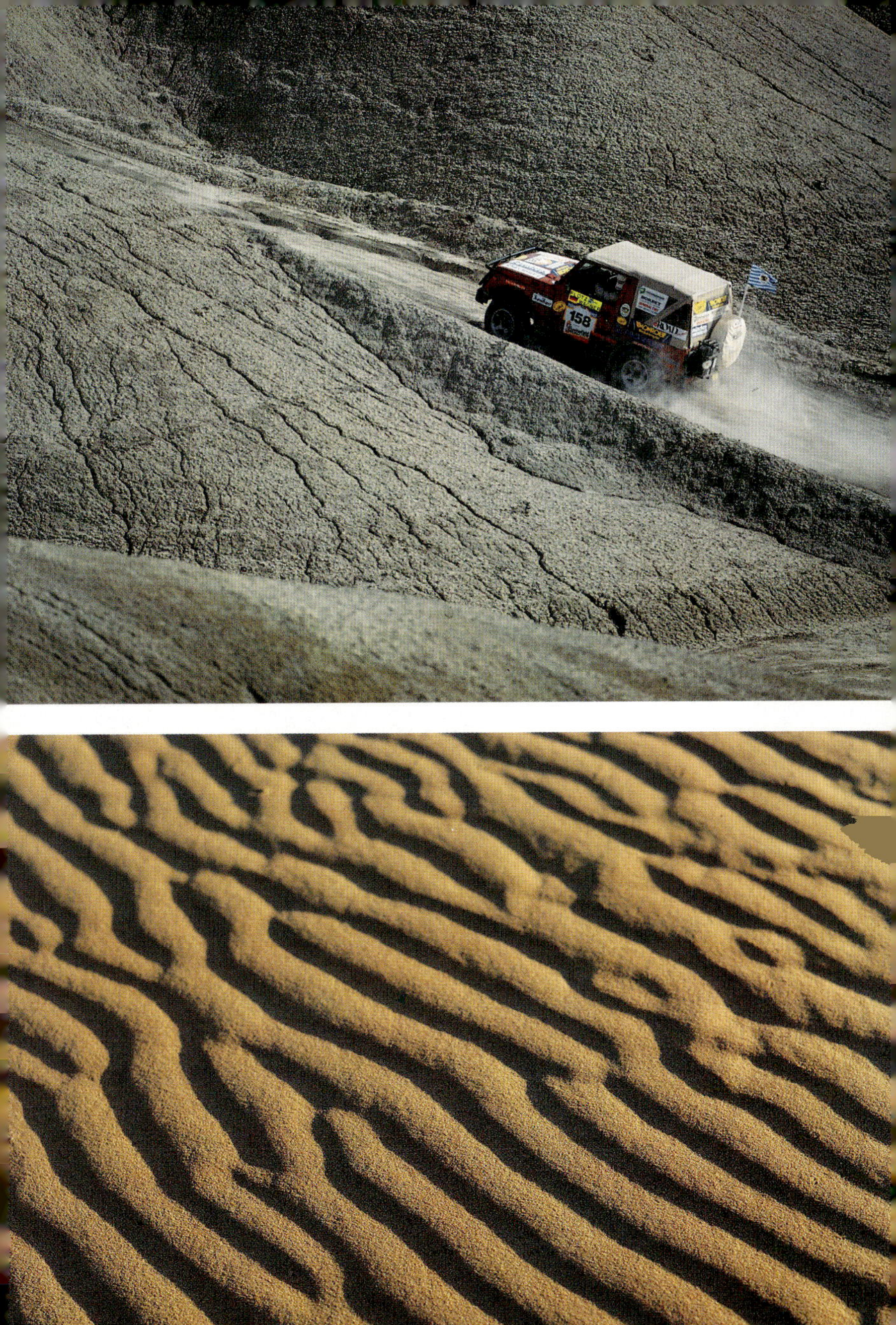

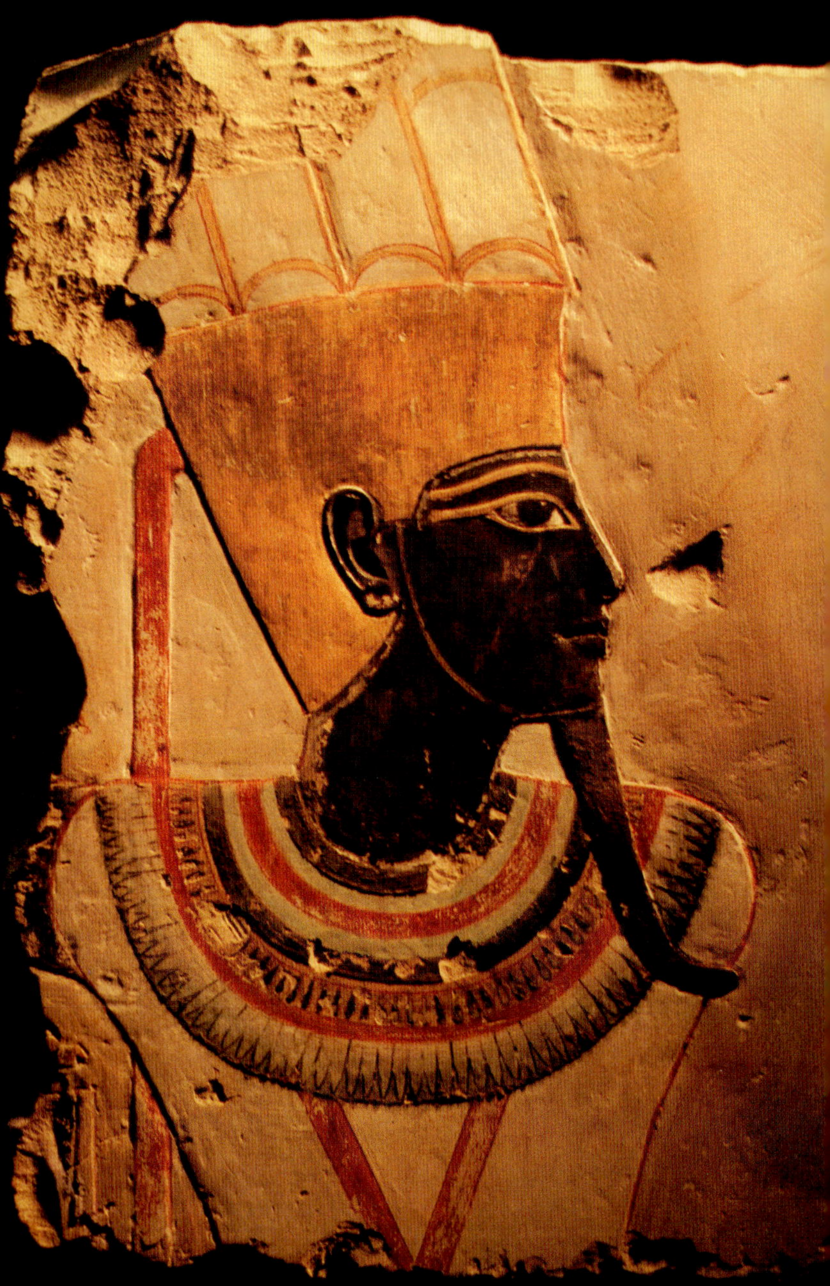

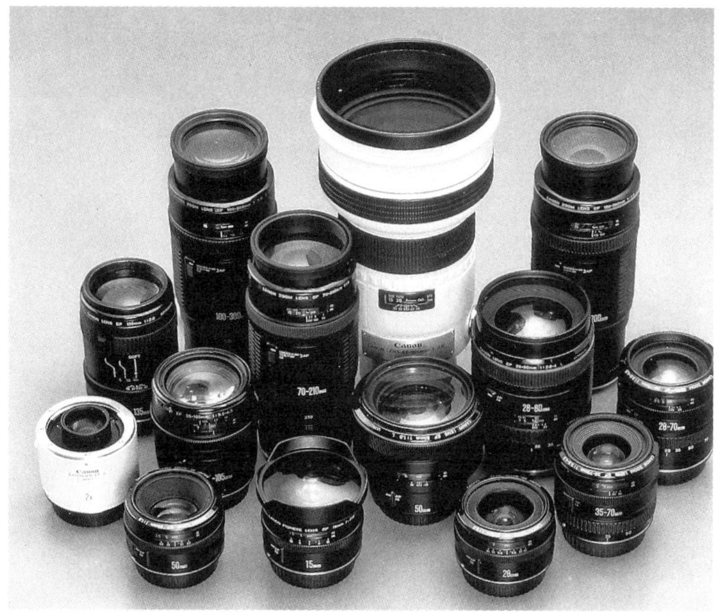

The Canon EF lens range is being constantly extended. It covers everything from fisheyes to special lenses for close-up shots and perspective compensation.

for architecture, or a fast 35mm or 50mm lens because you prefer to use available light instead of flash, or perhaps a macro for life size shots of insects or flowers.

Fixed Focal Lengths or Zoom Lenses?

Canon offer the right autofocus lenses for every purpose - by now more than thirty. These cover a range of focal lengths from 15mm to 600mm, without any gaps. The surprisingly high number of

The warm yellow tone in the photograph was created by the artificial lighting in the museum. Flashguns were not allowed and would have destroyed the atmosphere of the setting.

Lens	Focus Drive		Angle of View	Construction	Minimum Aperture	Closest Focusing Distance		Filter Size (mm)	Length		Weight	
	AFD	USM				(m)	(ft.)		(mm)	(in.)	(g)	(oz.)
Fish-Eye EF 15 mm f/2.8	●		180°	7-8	22	0.2	0.7	Filter Holder	62.2	2-7/16	330	11.6
EF 24 mm f/2.8	●		84°	10-10	22	0.25	0.8	58	48.5	1-15/16	270	9.5
EF 28 mm f/2.8	●		75°	5-5	22	0.3	1	52	42.5	1-11/16	185	6.5
EF 35 mm f/2	●		63°	5-7	22	0.25	0.8	52	42.5	1-11/16	210	7.4
EF 50 mm f/1.8 II	●		46°	5-6	22	0.45	1.5	52	41	1-5/8	130	4.6
EF 50 mm f/1 L (Ultrasonic)		●	46°	9-11	16	0.6	2	72	81.5	3-3/16	985	2.2 lb.
Compact-Macro EF 50 mm f/2.5	●		46°	8-9	32	0.23	0.75	52	63	2-1/2	280	9.9
EF 85 mm f/1.2 L (Ultrasonic)		●	28° 30'	7-8	16	0.95	3.1	72	84	3-5/16	1025	2.3 lb.
Macro EF 100 mm f/2.8	●		92°	9-10	32	0.31	1.02	52	105.5	4-1/8	650	22.9
Softfocus EF 135 mm f/2.8	●		18°	6-7	32	1.3	4.3	52	98.4	3-7/8	390	13.8
EF 200 mm f/1.8 L (Ultrasonic)		●	12°	10-12	22	2.5	8.2	48	208	8-3/16	3000	6.6 lb.
EF 300 mm f/2.8 L (Ultrasonic)		●	8° 15'	7-9	32	3	9.8	48	253	9-9/16	2855	6.3 lb.
EF 400 mm f/2.8 L (Ultrasonic)		●	6° 10'	9-11	32	4	13	48	348	13-11/16	6100	13.4 lb.
EF 600 mm f/4 L (Ultrasonic)		●	4° 10'	8-9	32	6	19.7	48	456	17-15/16	6000	13.2 lb.
EF 20-35 mm f/2.8 L	●		94°-63°	12-15	22	0.5	1.6	72	89	3-1/2	540	19.1
EF 28-70 mm f/3.5-4.5 II	●		75°-34°	9-10	22-29	0.39	1.3	52	75.6	3	285	10.1
EF 28-80 mm f/2.8-4 L (Ultrasonic)		●	75°-30°	11-15	22	0.5	1.6	72	119.5	4-11/16	945	2.1 lb.

Lens												
EF 35-70 mm f/3.5-4.5	●		63°-34°	8-9	22-29	0.39	1.3	52	63	2-1/2	245	8.6
EF 35-80 mm f/4-4.5	●		63°-30°	8-8	22-32	0.37	1.2	52	61	2-3/8	190	6.7
EF 35-105 mm f/3.5-4.5	●		63°-23° 20'	11-14	22-29	0.95	3.1	58	81.9	3-1/4	400	14.1
EF 35-105 mm f/4.5-5.6	●		63°-23° 30'	12-13	22-27	0.85	2.8	58	63	2-1/2	280	9.9
EF 35-135 mm f/4-5.6 (Ultrasonic)		●	63°-18°	12-14	22-32	0.75	2.5	58	86.4	3-3/8	425	15.0
EF 70-210 mm f/3.5-4.5 (Ultrasonic)		●	34°-11° 20'	10-14	27-32	1.2	3.9	58	121.5	4-3/4	550	19.4
EF 75-300 mm f/4-5.6	●		32° 11' -8° 15'	9-13	32-45	1.5	4.9	58	122	4-13/16	500	17.7
EF 80-200 mm f/2.8 L	●		30°-12°	13-16	32	1.8	5.9	72	185.7	7-5/16	1330	2.9 lb.
EF 80-200 mm f/4.5-5.6	●		30°-12°	7-10	22-27	1.5	4.9	52	77.8	3-1/16	265	9.3
EF 100-300 mm f/5.6 L	●		24°-8° 15'	10-15	32	1.5	4.9	58	166.6	6-9/16	695	24.5
EF 100-300 mm f/4.5-5.6 (Ultrasonic)		●	24°-8° 15'	10-13	32	1.5	4.9	58	121.5	4-3/4	540	19.1
Extender EF 2X	–	–	–	5-7	–	–	–	–	50.5	2	240	8.5
Extender EF 1.4X	–	–	–	4-5	–	–	–	–	27.3	1-1/16	200	7.1
Life-Size Converter EF	–	–	–	3-4	–	–	–	–	34.9	1-3/8	160	5.6
TS E 24/3.5 L	–	–	84°	9-11	22	0.3	1	72	86.8	3-7/16	570	20.1
TS E 45/2.8	–	–	51°	9-10	22	0.4	1.4	72	90	3-9/16	645	22.8
TS E 90/2.8	–	–	27°	5-6	32	0.5	1.6	58	88	3-7/16	565	19.9

● Extender EF 2X is for exclusive use with EF 200 mm f/1.8 L, EF 300 mm f/2.8 L and EF 400 mm f/2.8 L. ● Extender EF 1.4X is for exclusive use with EF 200 mm f/1.8 L, EF 300 mm f/2.8 L, EF 400 mm f/2.8 L and EF 600 mm f/4 L. ● Life-Size Converter EF is for exclusive use with Compact-Macro EF 50 mm f/2.5.
All data are based on Canon's Standard Test Method. Subject to change without notice.

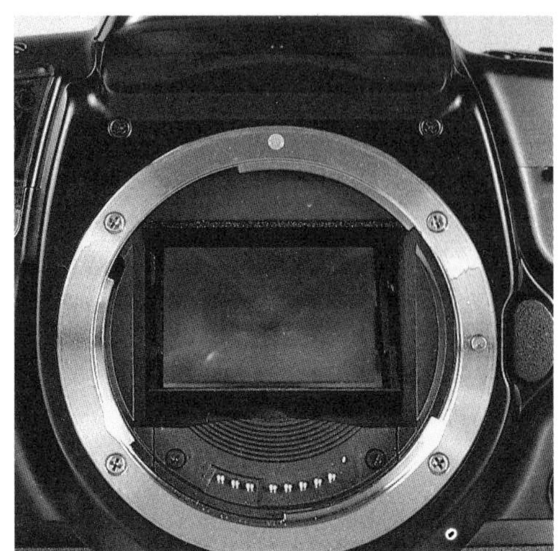

Compared to the FD bayonet, the Canon EF bayonet is bigger, making possible the construction of larger lenses which are of particular benefit to reporters and sports and animal photographers.

variable focal length lenses, generally known as zooms, may seem strange or at least unusual to many traditional photographers, but the whole EOS EF lens range is based on a recognisable strategy. The EOS 1000 philosophy is based on its use with zoom lenses, although EOS 1000 owners are perfectly at liberty to use fixed focal length lenses from the EF range if they wish.

Canon offer a range of zoom lenses, starting at 28mm or 35mm focal length and reaching up to 70mm or 135mm; then there are tele zooms, starting from 50mm and 100mm focal length and reaching up to 200mm or 300mm. These can be considered the standard EOS range, which is most popular in the field of general amateur photography. Two or three zoom lenses can cope with almost every photographic task.

For professionals and amateur photographers looking for professional quality and the highest possible performance, Canon offer five high-quality zoom lenses which carry the designation "L" and fully cover the focal length range from 20mm to 300mm. These zoom lenses can be complemented with a series of extremely fast fixed focal length lenses, which can satisfy every EOS owner.

94

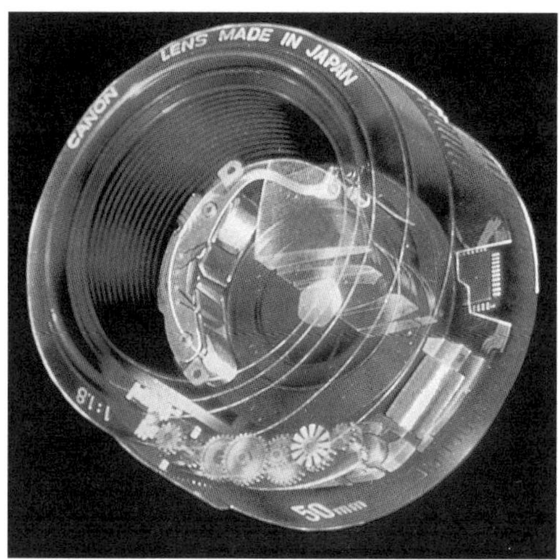

The Canon EF lenses are distinguished from most other autofocus lenses by the integral focusing motor.

The question of zoom versus fixed focal length no longer applies. Apart from one or two exceptions - which are recognisable by their price - all the negative characteristics associated with zoom lenses for years have been reduced to a minimum. Even with the cheapest short focal lengths, pin cushion distortion or vignetting are normally rare.

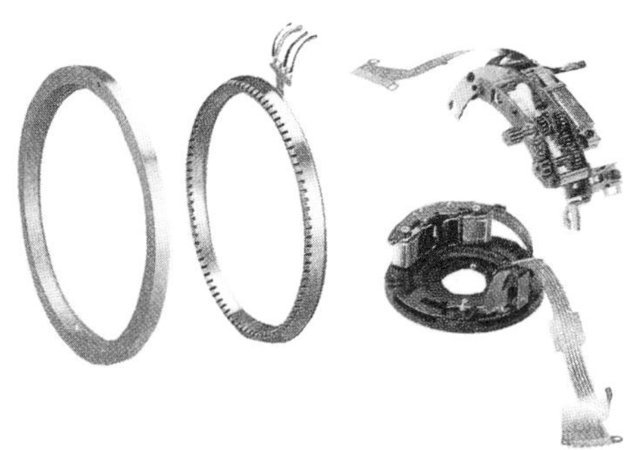

New techniques from Canon: the ultrasonic AF motor and the electromagnetic aperture control system.

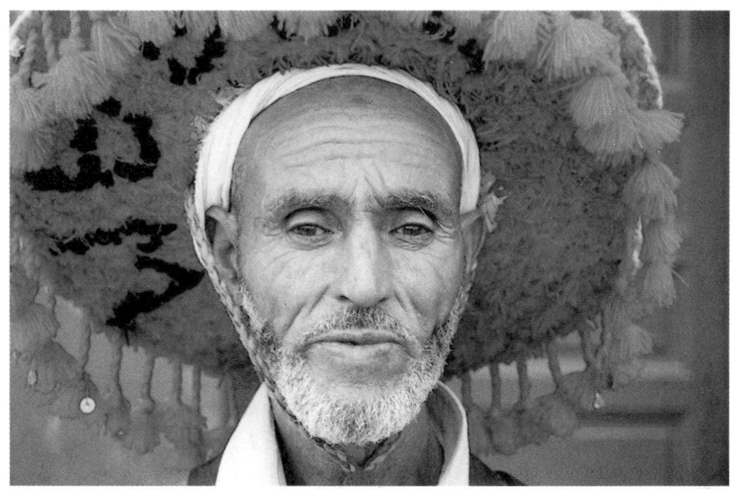

Excellent character studies can be achieved with medium focal length telephoto lenses, from approximately 80mm focal length.

The main disadvantage of many zoom lenses remains their relatively low speed. This isn't a problem peculiar to Canon, but applies equally to zoom lenses from all manufacturers. On the other hand, the conditions for the use of zoom lenses have been improved by a considerable increase in film speeds at the same time as improvements in grain and sharpness.

Reflections are always appealing. This subject is made by the many different frames.

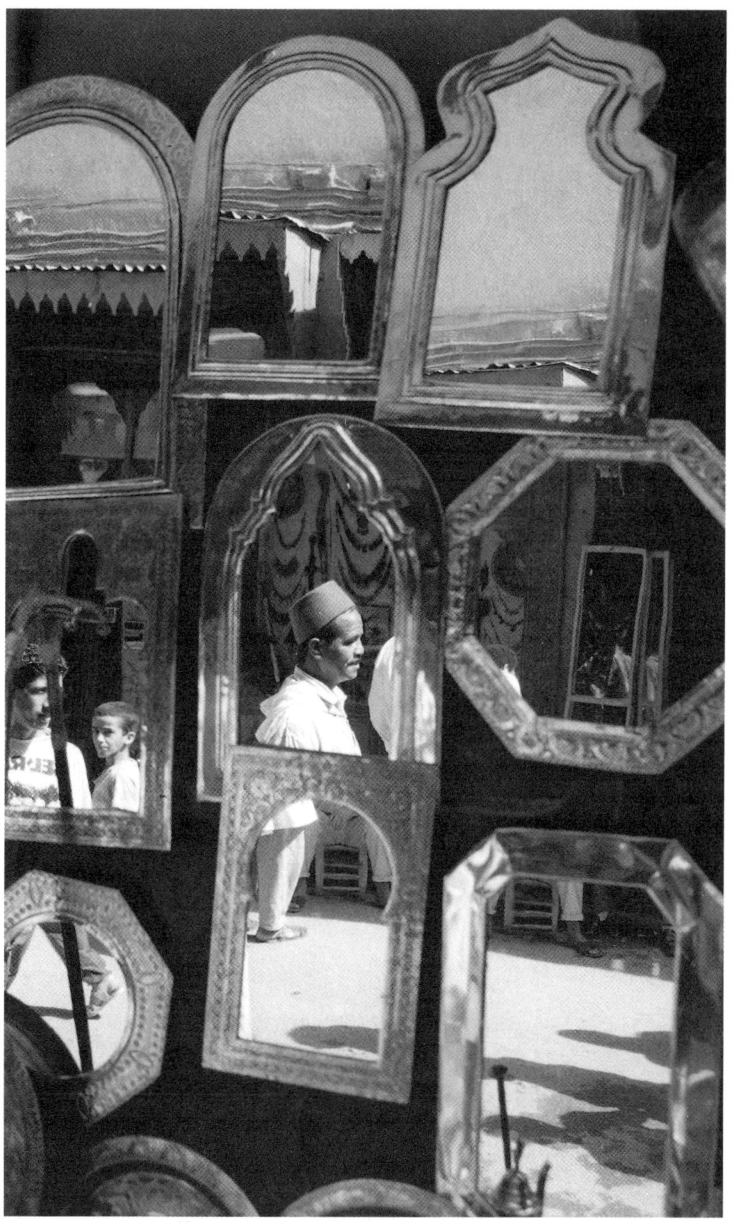

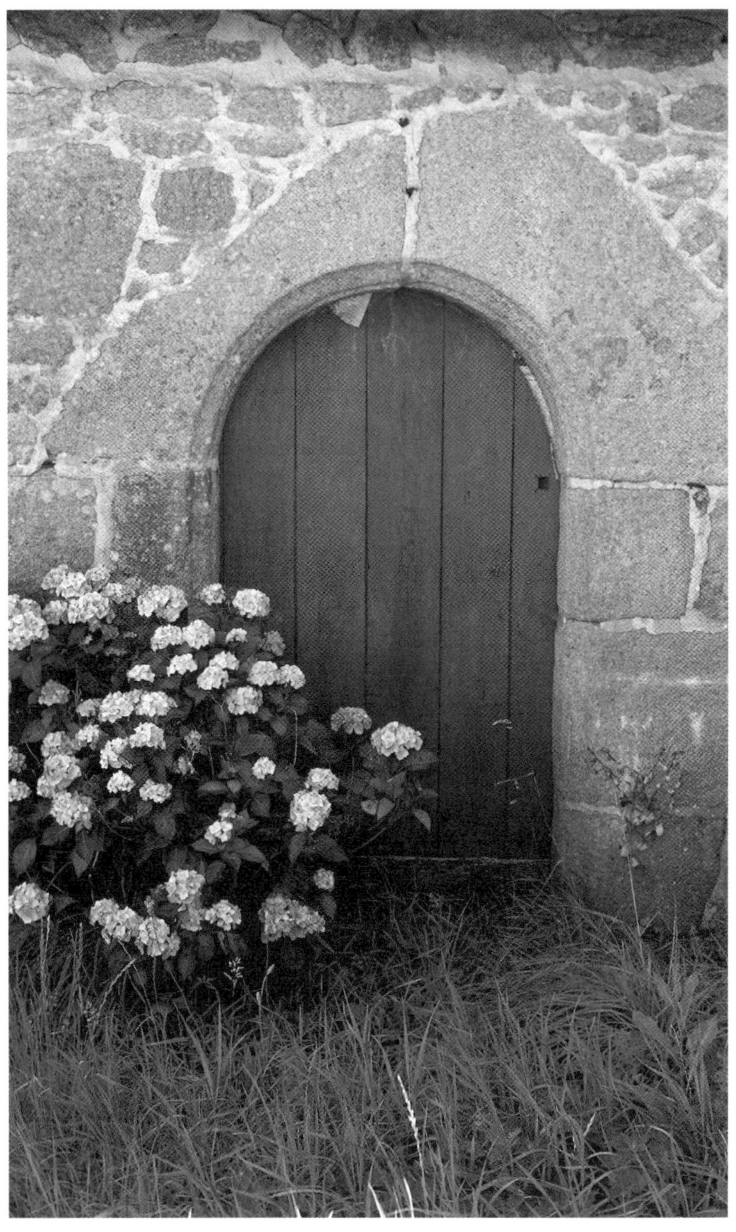

EF Lenses Suitable for the EOS 1000

Zoom Lenses

The EF zoom lenses have two different ways of changing the focal length. There are rotary zooms and slide zooms.

Canon have developed a fairly simple design for zoom lenses, and this design now delivers inexpensive zoom lenses which are surprising in their quality and compactness. This is a so-called two-group construction which facilitates the production of very compact zoom lenses even in the wide-angle range. The front half of the lens takes on the jobs of changing the focal length and focusing, whereas the rear half acts as a compensator between the changes in focus and the focal length. The advantage is that the element groups at the front remain relatively small. The correction of image faults is easier than on zoom lenses built in the four group design. There is hardly any barrel-shaped distortion at short focal lengths. The only disadvantage is that the focal length range has to remain relatively small. The focal length is changed by rotating a ring on the lens barrel, which is why they are called rotary zooms.

Where longer setting distances are available, for example in the telephoto range, the focal length can be changed with a sliding ring. In the Canon EF system this applies to lenses which start in the wide-angle range.

From the 35mm wide-angle focal length to the 105mm telephoto setting, the subject increases in size by a factor of 3 from a constant shooting distance. From 35mm to 135mm this factor is 3.8. This facilitates a portrait shot in the telephoto range, and a full length shot of the same person in the wide-angle setting. The portrait shot was deliberately the first to be mentioned. Experience has shown that it makes sense to set every zoom to its longest focal length to start with. As soon as you look through the camera and the image becomes sharp in the viewfinder, you will have the largest possible image. In snapshot situations you should take a photograph immediately; you will then be able to change your angle and decide whether there is a better image section. This will be the case only rarely, and then often at the other end of the focal length range. When shortening the focal length, the distance setting is only changed in exceptional circumstances; this happens more frequently if you work the other way around.

For many subjects, especially on holiday, or if you don't want to carry any additional lenses, a focal length range between 35mm and 80mm or 105mm, is ideal in some 90% of situations. This means that you will not only get your subjects at the desired reproduction scale with just one lens; you also get the chance to be creative with the focal length.

The wide-angle range offers a panoramic view for landscapes. It helps to fit larger groups of people into the frame, and it helps to solve crowded conditions for indoor shots.

A focal length around 80mm is the ideal focal length for shots of people, snapshots at parties, sporting activities and photographs of children and animals.

Many zoom lenses have a so-called macro setting. This doesn't replace a special macro lens for really close-up work because the macro setting relies on sharpness only at the centre of the image, and sufficient stopping down is therefore a prerequisite for best results. The autofocus works here as well and has a separate setting ranging from macro to infinity. The seemingly reduced distance range of the lens is nevertheless its real working range and should therefore be chosen all the time, if only in order to avoid unnecessary focusing movement.

The shortest focusing distance varies from lens to lens, and the normal autofocus range is between this distance and infinity.

Canon EF 35-80mm,f/4-5.6
This lens was designed specifically for the EOS 1000. Its optical construction, which offers an angle of view between 63° and 30° along the diagonal, consists of 8 separate elements. Fast focusing

takes place with a new type of motor which is extremely small. Depending on the selected focal length, the minimum aperture is between f/22 and f/32. The shortest focusing distance is 37cm. The reproduction scale in the 35mm wide-angle setting is 1:8.33 (subject area 20x30cm), in the 80mm telephoto setting it is 1:4, with a postcard-sized subject area of 96x144mm. The filter size is 52mm. As the filter turns during focusing, polarising filters can only be set effectively once focusing has taken place. The zoom is just 61mm long and has a diameter of 68.6mm. The glass fibre-strengthened plastics used for the lens casing reduce the weight to exactly 190g.

Canon EF 35-105mm,f/4.5-5.6

This new lens for the EOS 1000 was announced at the time of going to press. It extends the focusing range by a useful 25mm into the medium telephoto range, compared with the 35-80mm. The design employs a moulded aspherical element. This very compact lens is almost one-third lighter than the well-established 35-105mm lens.

Canon EF 28-70mm,f/3.5-4.5 II

This lens offers an extension into the wide-angle range. It is practically free from flare because of an iris diaphragm which, at a constant aperture, can move between the front and rear element groups. Ten elements in 9 groups provide a variable angle of view between 75° and 34°. The arch-type motor can focus from infinity to 50cm in 0.36 sec. Depending on the focal length this gives a smallest subject area between 34.8x52.5cm and 14x22.5cm. These figures become smaller still in the 39cm macro setting. The smallest aperture of this lens is between f/22 and f/29. It is 75.6mm long and weighs 285g.

Telephoto Zoom Lenses

The advantage of choosing the desired and ideal image section without changing the shooting distance is tempting - even if it means that many photographers stop paying attention to the ideal shooting distance, simply because they can zoom in on, or away from, their image section. But the relationship between foreground and background is quite different if the distance is 20m and the focal length 200mm to that at 8m and with a focal length of 80mm. This is not noticeable in the main subject, but in the size and sharpness of the background, as well as its visual relationship with the subject. Many photographers think and see in fixed focal lengths; they have a 50mm, 100mm and 200mm mode. They know in advance what the shot is supposed to look like, and what the relationship between foreground and background is going to be. A zoom lens slows down this learning process, but it also offers other creative possibilities, as for example the so-called zoom effect.

The focal length range from about 80mm to 200mm is the most popular. Canon has increased the range further still - to 50mm on the shorter side and up to 300mm in the telephoto range.

There is a total of eleven zoom lenses ranging between 50mm and 300mm in focal length; three with the additional 'L' marking, two of the cheaper USM lenses, and two developed specially for the EOS 1000.

Canon EF 80-200mm,f/4.5-5.6

This lens designed specifically for the EOS 1000 should cover most requirements in the long focal length range. It has a diagonal angle of view of between 30° and 12°. Set at 200mm, every subject detail is four times larger than it appears to the human eye. Ten elements in 7 groups produce an image of surprisingly high quality in the range from infinity to 1.5m. The largest reproduction scale at 80mm is 1:15.38, giving a subject area of 37x58cm. At 200m a reproduction scale of 1:6.4 means that a subject area of 152x225mm - A5 size - can be shot to fill the frame.

Canon EF 75-300,f/4-5.6

This new lens for the EOS 1000 was announced as this book went to press. With its extended range to 300mm it is even more versatile than the 80-200mm, and also slightly faster at the 75mm end.

Standard Focal Lengths

Normal or standard lenses have a focal length which roughly corresponds to the length of the image diagonal. In the 35mm format this is around 43mm. So everything with a focal length between 40mm and 55mm falls into this category. But for optical and production reasons a standard value of 50mm has been preferred since the beginnings of 35mm photography.

Three lenses with a focal length of 50mm are available for EOS cameras, but only one of these is a standard lens. Of the other two, one is a macro lens because it has a particularly good close-up performance, the other is a specialist lens for very low-light situations and will not leave you much change out of £1500.

All three lenses have an angle of view (along the diagonal) of 46° and the effects which can be achieved with this angle roughly correspond to what is seen by the human eye. Even if a zoom lens usually takes on the job of a standard lens with the EOS 1000, there are several reasons why you shouldn't necessarily do without a normal lens.

Canon EF 50mm,f/1.8

The difference in speed between a small zoom lens and a standard lens with f/1.8 almost corresponds to a difference of two aperture stops. Translated into shutter speed, this corresponds to a difference of, say, $^1/_{15}$ sec and $^1/_{50}$ sec. So we are back within the rule about the reciprocal value for shots without camera shake blur. This is how much difference there is between the EF 50mm,f/1.8 and all zoom lenses with the same focal length. Used with a fast film, f/1.8 can do without a flash in the theatre or the circus and, with its maximum aperture, can also be successful in museums and churches.

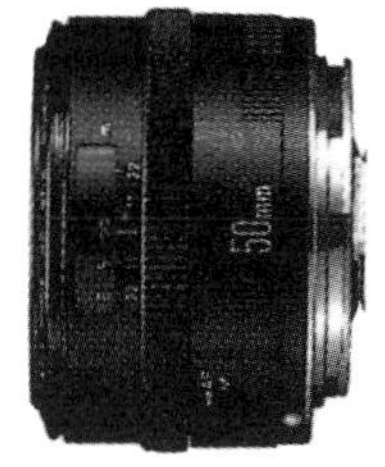
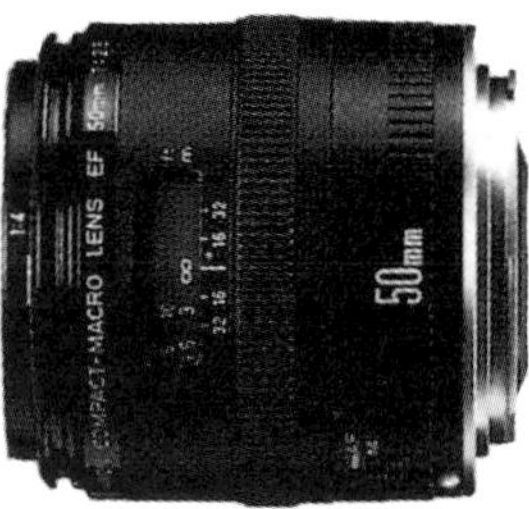

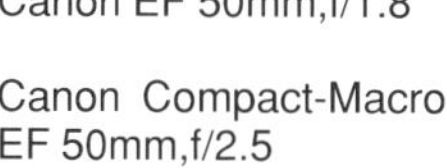

Canon EF 50mm,f/1.8

Canon Compact-Macro
EF 50mm,f/2.5

The shortest focusing distance of the standard lens is 45cm, giving a reproduction scale of 1:15. This means that the smallest subject area is 36x24cm, a little smaller than a sheet of A3 paper.

Its optical construction consists of 6 elements in 5 groups. Focusing takes place automatically with an arch-type motor, or can be controlled manually. The focusing speed from infinity to the shortest focusing distance is 0.44 sec. The minimum aperture is f/22 and the filter size 52mm. The filter does not turn with the lens. The standard lens is just 42.5mm long and weighs only 190g.

Canon Compact-Macro EF 50mm,f/2.5
This macro lens, which is also suitable as a standard lens, has an optical construction of 9 elements in 8 groups. Its arch-type motor can focus automatically from infinity to a reproduction scale of 0.5 in 1.5 sec, but it can also be focused manually. The lens is 63mm long and weighs 285g.

Every lens has optimum correction for a certain distance range. At a distance of 50cm the standard 50mm,f/1.8 lens can still produce an acceptable image but, where precision is important, the loss of performance of the normal lens becomes detectable. There are special lenses which deliver top performance for technical and scientific applications, such as copying and duplication. With the 50mm macro lens the emphasis is on high resolution, excellent contrast and flatness of field. This is achieved with a symmetrical lens construction and floating elements. The shortest focusing distance is 23cm, where the subject is reproduced on the film at half its real size. The focusing distance of 23cm is the distance between the subject and the focal plane. On the EOS 1000 the focal plane is situated roughly at the rear edge of the LCD panel.

When shooting flowers, insects or other small subjects from nature, it makes sense to use the aperture-priority or the depth-of-field program. The latter program signals that the required depth of field area cannot be realised, by flashing the minimum aperture of f/32. A clever choice of image area cannot completely get around the problems of small depth of field which, with a reproduction scale of 1:2 and an aperture of f/11, is barely 6mm, but it can at least reduce those problems to an acceptable level.

This can be done, for example, by focusing on a flower in such a way that it is parallel to the focal plane.

If you're looking for a precise reproduction scale, you should switch to manual mode and set the scale with the manual focusing ring.

The 4-element EF life-size converter, also known as the EF macro converter, is meant to be used only with this lens. An electronic block for all other lenses prevents misuse. This converter, which is placed between the camera body and the lens, allows shots with a reproduction scale of between 1:4 and 1:1 and compensates for the spherical aberration of this remarkably fast standard lens in the close-up and macro range.

Wide-angle Lenses

The 'much more subject in the shot' possibilities of wide-angle lenses cause problems for many photographers, if they are overpowered by the crowded image in the viewfinder and don't pay the necessary attention to every subject detail.

Wide-angle lenses have a distinct characteristic spatial effect. This starts surprisingly close to the camera.

The 24mm focal length will give you strong spatial effects, but without the considerable distortion of the subject towards the edge of the shot and the extreme emphasis on the foreground you get with shorter focal lengths. This focal length is equally suitable for landscape and interior shots.

The angle of view of a focal length around 28mm is considered normal these days, and the subject area to be covered with it can even be lit by the Speedlite 200E flash unit. With a little thought and practice this focal length can be used in such a way that only an expert would notice the wide-angle effect. But it is also possible to do the reverse. By cleverly emphasising the foreground you can draw attention to the spatial depth.

For some people a focal length of 35mm is already comparable with a standard lens, and the typical wide-angle effects only appear in a few applications, such as photo journalism or portrait photography.

The designs of the Canon 24mm and 28mm focal lengths have proved to be excellent over the years, and have simply been updated with the latest technical improvements in order to be used with the EOS range. It should be noted that the 24mm lens has its optimum correction at just four metres; this is because the designers have worked on the assumption that, at infinity, focusing rarely takes place through direct setting, but mostly through the depth of field. The shortest focusing distance is 25cm on the 24mm lens and 30cm on the 28mm. Good reproduction quality is provided by floating elements. Whether the 24mm or the 28mm makes more sense is mostly a question of photographic mentality, but as the standard zoom includes the 35mm focal length, the 24mm lens can become a real super wide-angle alternative.

Canon EF 24mm,f/2.8

The design consists of 10 elements, one of them aspherical, to increase the reproduction quality particularly in the short distance range. The angle of view is 84°. At the shortest focusing distance this provides a subject area of 18.5x27.7cm. The focusing speed is 0.44 sec. This super wide-angle lens is just 48mm long and weighs 270g.

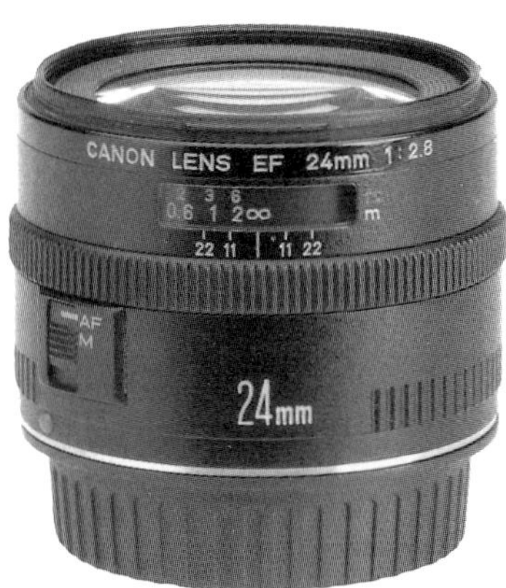

Canon EF 24mm,f/2.8 - sooner or later this lens is a must for every friend of a wide angle of view.

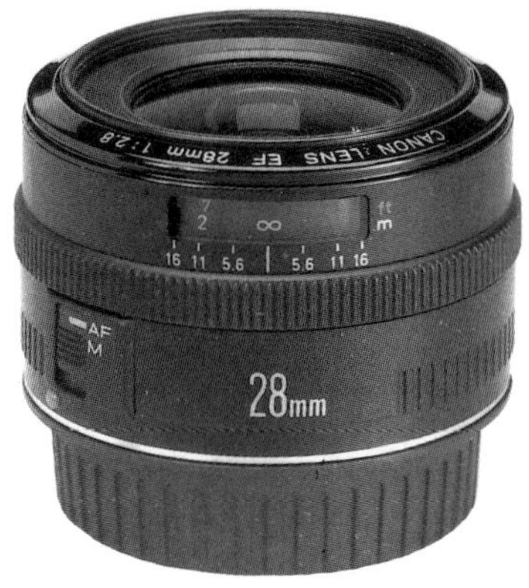

Canon EF 28mm,f/2.8 - an all-round wide-angle lens.

The Canon EF 28mm,f/2.8

This lens has 5 elements, one of them aspherical. At an angle of view of 75° and a shortest focusing distance of 30cm, the smallest subject area is 18.5x22.7cm. The AFD motor focuses from infinity to the shortest focusing distance in 0.44 sec. The lens is 42.5mm long and weighs just 185g.

Medium Telephoto Lenses

There are two special medium telephoto lenses which you might need in addition to the telephoto zoom, or instead of it, depending on your photographic interests. The 100mm macro lens enables close-up shots to be taken of flowers, insects or small animals from a greater shooting distance than the 50mm macro. This might be essential if you want to avoid frightening your subject or trampling a habitat. The 135mm softfocus is of special interest to portrait photographers or for taking dreamy landscapes.

Canon Macro EF 100mm,f/2.8

This fast macro lens gives close-up shots up to a scale of 1:1, without an additional accessory. A focus limitation allows a choice

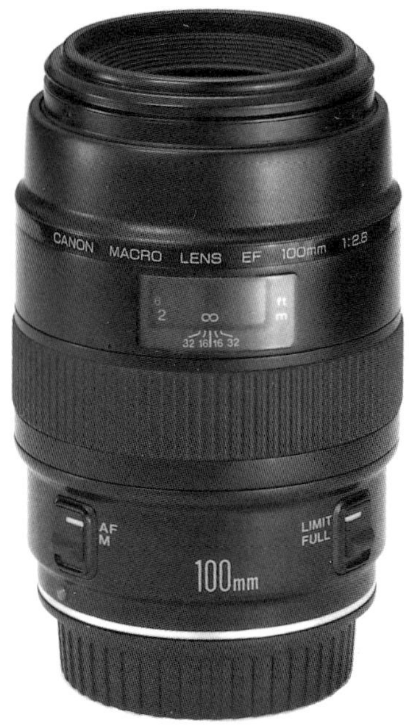

Canon Macro EF 100mm, f/2.8 - its longer focal length offers favourable shooting distances for shots of small animals. Lighting the macro subject is also easier than with the 50mm lens, and in addition, no converter is necessary for shots in the reproduction ratio of 1:1.

of two distance ranges; one in the macro range between 0.31m and 0.57m, the other from 0.57m to infinity. The focusing motor manages this distance in exactly one second. The smallest subject area is 24x36mm. Ten elements in 9 groups give an angle of view of 24°. The lens is 105.5mm long and weighs 650g.

Canon Softfocus EF 135mm, f/2.8

This is a soft-focus lens offering a diffusion effect in addition to the normal focus setting. Continuously variable degrees of softness can be selected. This effect is most pronounced when set at 2; set at 0 it is switched off altogether. As the optical construction includes an aspherical moulded glass element, the soft-focus effect does not have the usual aberrations. Whether automatic or manual, focusing should take place after the degree of soft focus has been selected. But as it is not easy to recognize sharpness precisely in a shot with soft focus, it is probably just as well to leave the job of focusing to the camera.

The soft-focus effect, which is achieved by de-focusing one of the elements, depends on the combination of aperture and soft-focus setting. A selection of setting 2 and f/2.8 produces the softest effect; at f/5.6 the soft focus is lost completely.

Subjects photographed against the light lend themselves well to soft-focus moods, but only if they are not lit too harshly. Very strong and harsh backlighting should not be photographed with the strongest soft-focus setting, but at a maximum setting of 1.

Highlights and side light give the best effect. They are particularly impressive against a dark background. A positive exposure compensation usually helps to increase the romantic touch.

Landscapes in spring, flowers and, of course, portraits are suitable subjects for soft focus photography. This specialist lens is useful whenever you want to create romantic moods.

The soft-focus lens consists of 7 elements in 6 groups and has a focal length of 135mm. It can also produce normal sharpness. In landscape photography typical long distance perspective becomes noticeable, whereas the 135mm focal length is sufficient to guarantee a clean separation of subject and background in portrait photography.

The arch-type motor of this medium focal length telephoto lens focuses from infinity to 1.3m in 0.39 sec. At this distance the subject area is 19.3x29cm. The minimum aperture is f/32. The soft-focus ring has two settings, and the soft-focus effect is achieved by moving an aspherical element along the optical axis. In this way the correction of spherical aberration is maintained. The lens is just under 10cm long and weighs 390g.

The Rest of Canon's Armoury

In the previous section I described the lenses you are most likely to use with the Canon Eos 1000, including some specially designed for the camera, but they represent less than half the Canon EF lenses available for EOS cameras. Most of the rest are really for professionals, or amateurs with very special interests, and are very expensive.

However, you never know when you might get the opportunity to borrow one, or how your photographic hobby might develop, and for that reason the other EF lenses are described here.

There are many more interesting zooms, including some superb ones of the "L" type and some faster by a whole stop. There are also some specialist fixed focus lenses, such as a fish-eye and the very fast EF 50mm, f/1 USM and EF 85mm, f/1.2 L USM.

If in the future you trade up to, say, an EOS 1, then these lenses might be what tempts you.

Canon EF 20-35mm,f/2.8 L

This one zoom lens, with the fast speed of f/2.8 over its entire focal length range, covers the entire wide-angle area. Internal focusing and the use of an aspherical element and of a floating elements system guarantee sharp reproduction at every focusing distance and focal length.

15 elements in 12 groups produce a diagonal angle of view from 94° to 63° (vertically 62° to 38°, horizontally 84° to 54°). The focusing distance ranges from infinity to 50cm. The focal length of the lens is changed by rotating an adjustable ring. This is also one of the technical reasons why this lens has an arch-type motor rather than an ultrasonic one. When you use this highly professional lens with your EOS 1000, make sure the camera is always perfectly aligned, so that vertical lines remain vertical, and

---

On shots like this the camera has to cope with the brightness of the background as well as the darkness of the stone.

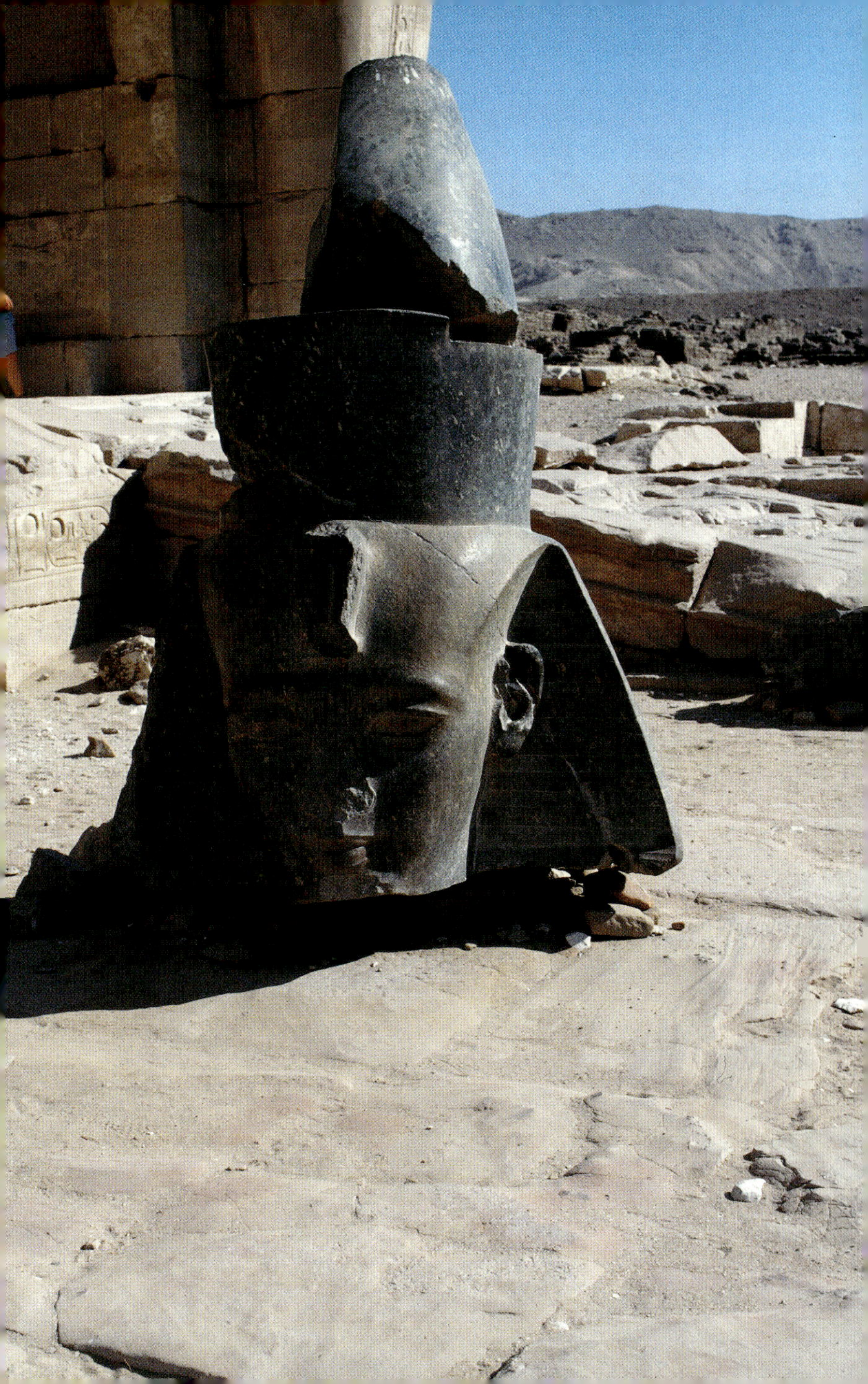

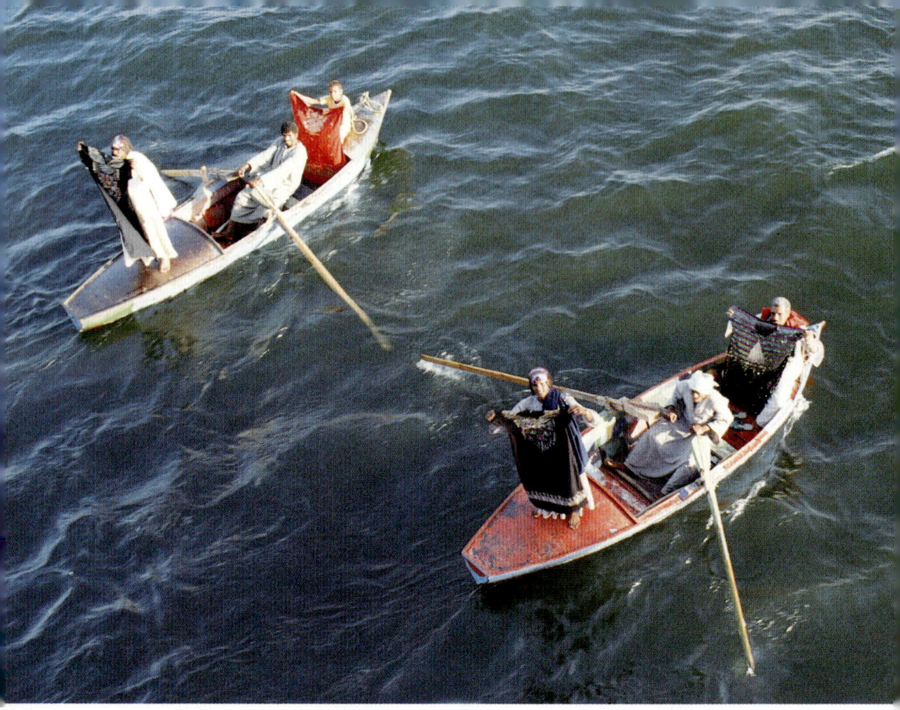

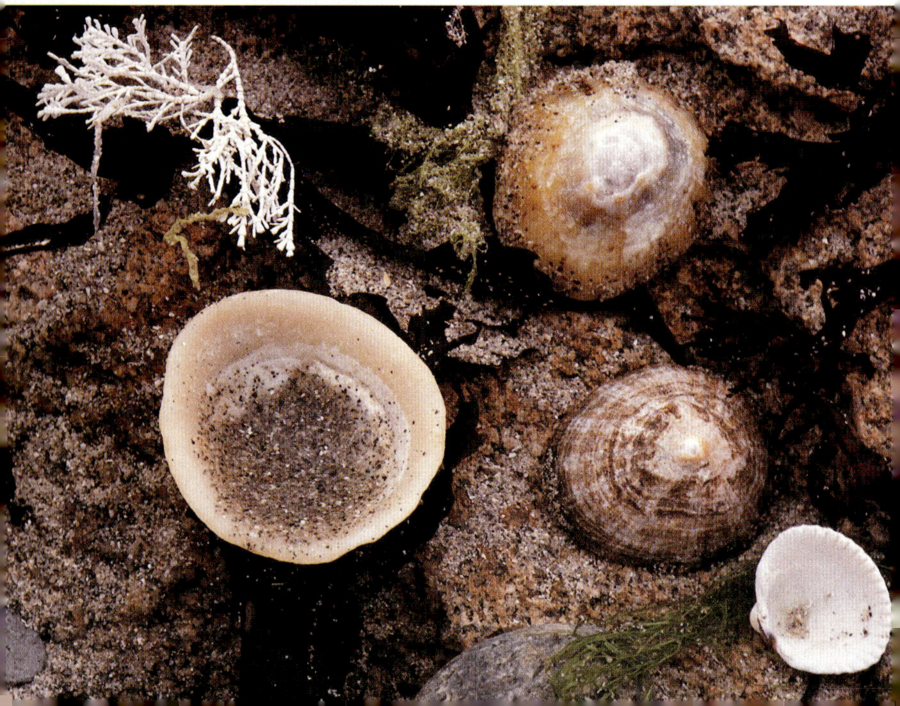

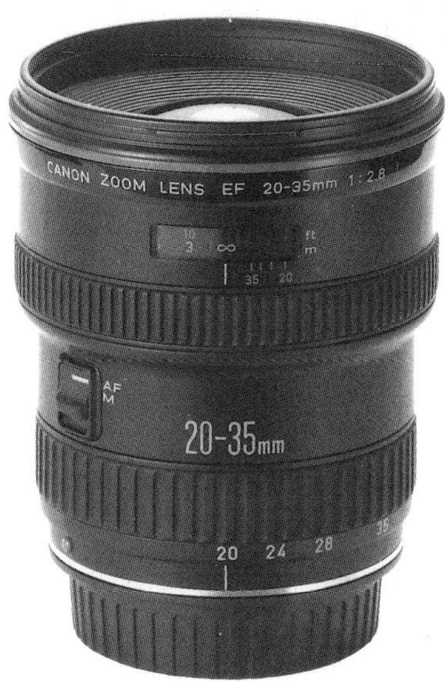

The Canon EF 20-35mm,f/2.8 L - a zoom which covers the wide-angle range and offers a high speed.

horizontals don't appear crooked. If you sometimes have problems aligning the camera precisely, you should attach a mini spirit-level to the accessory shoe.

Converging lines are, of course, no more a lens fault than the reproduction of spherical objects as ellipses at the edge of a shot taken with a 20mm focal length. For those reasons, you should never place people on the edge of your shot if you have selected a very wide-angle setting. If you have use one or other super wide-angle lens in order to overcome space problems in a group shot, note the following; the people on the left- and right-hand edge of the shot should stand at least one metre further back than those in the centre of the shot.

Canon EF 28-80mm,f/2.8-4 L USM

Two aspherical elements provide an astonishing performance throughout the entire, rather large, focal length range of this 3x zoom with ultrasonic motor. The optical construction consists of 15 elements in 11 groups. You can select an angle of view between

Picture composition with different lenses. With an 80mm setting (top); with the Macro EF 100mm,f/2.8 (bottom).

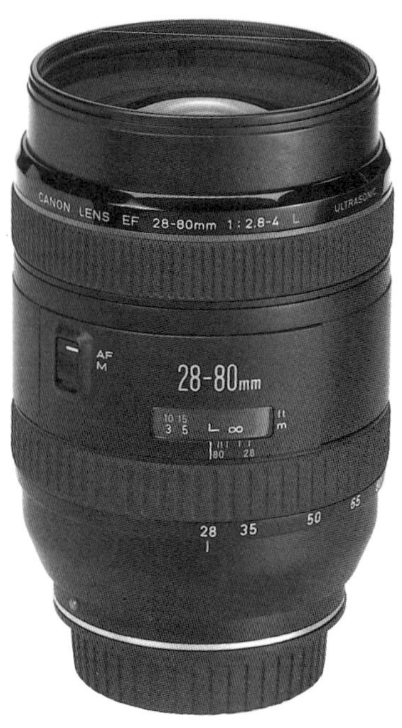

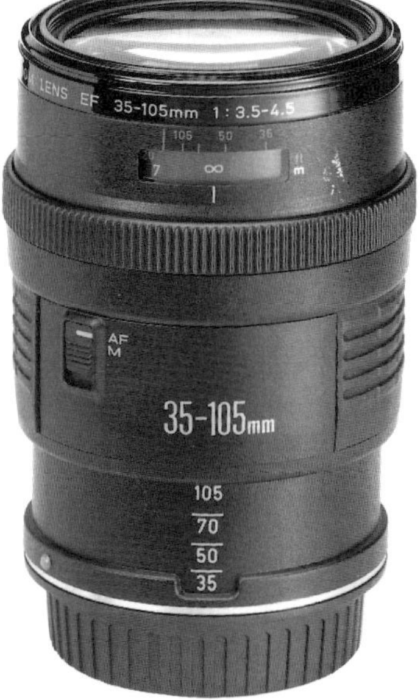

(top left)
Canon EF 28-80mm,f/2.8-4 L USM offers all wide-angle focal lengths and reaches up to portrait telephoto.

(right and bottom)
Canon EF 35-105mm,f/3.5-4.5 and Canon EF 100-300mm,f/5.6 - a zoom pair for universal use.

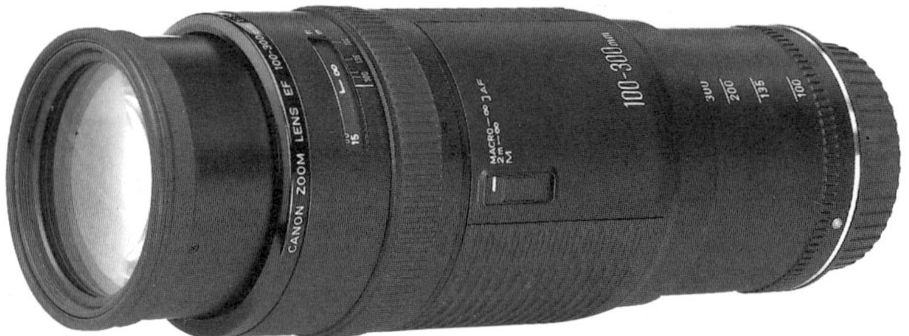

75° and 30°, and focusing from infinity to 75cm takes exactly 1 sec. This gives a subject area between 53.3x80cm and 20x30cm, which is almost the same size as a sheet of A4 paper. In the macro setting at a distance of 50cm, the subject area is between 32x48cm and 12x18cm. The lens is just under 12cm long and 55g short of one kilo.

Canon EF 35-70mm,f/3.5-4.5

This is a light, compact zoom lens with an optical construction of 9 elements in 8 groups, giving an angle of view between 63° and 34°. The arch-type motor can traverse the entire focusing range, from infinity to 50cm, in 0.41 sec. This provides a subject area between 29.6x44.4cm and 16x24cm; in the macro setting of 39cm, the figures are between 22x33cm and 12x18cm. This zoom is barely 63mm long and weighs just 245g. The data for the lens with the additional A marking are identical, except that the manual focusing mode is missing. This reduces the weight by 15g to 230g.

Canon EF 35-105mm,f/3.5-4.5

This lens consists of 14 elements in 11 groups. You can select an angle of view between 63° and 23° 30'. The arch-type motor can cover the whole focusing range in 0.4 sec.

At a shortest focusing distance of 1.2 metres the subject area is between 66.6x100cm and 23.3x34.9cm. In the macro setting of 95cm the figures are between 43.6x65.4 and 15x22.5cm. This is the first inexpensive lens for discerning amateur photographers which combines the technology of aspherical lenses, internal focusing and a new inexpensive ultrasonic motor.

Canon EF 35-135mm,f/4.5-5.6 USM

This high quality standard zoom is particularly compact and light. It consists of 14 elements in 12 groups, including an aspherical lens. Fast internal focusing facilitates focusing from infinity to 1m in just 0.5 sec. Manual focusing is possible without switching off the autofocus. As with the other latest-generation lenses, the distance and reproduction scale are fed into the camera computer in order to control automatically the program modes, such as portrait and close-up. The smallest subject area is between 61.8x92.7mm and 21.3x32cm at 1m distance. In the macro setting the shortest focusing distance is reduced by a factor of 0.25, and the size of the subject area is reduced by the same factor. The zoom lens is less than 9cm long and weighs just 425g.

Canon EF 50-200mm,f/3.5-4.5
Canon EF 50-200mm,f/3.5-4.5 L

The construction provides consistent results across the whole focal length range. The optical construction comprises 16 elements in 13 groups, and 16 elements in 14 groups respectively. The latter includes a fluorite element which provides the additional L marking. The angle of view of both lenses ranges from 47° 42' to 12° 19'. The slide zoom focuses from infinity to 1.2m in 0.89 sec.

The smallest subject area in the telephoto range is 13.3x20cm, in the normal range it is 40x60cm. In the macro range, at 50cm shooting distance, the subject area is between 30x45cm and 10x15cm (postcard size). The minimum aperture is f/22 and f/29 respectively. The first figure always refers to the shortest focal length, the second to the longest. The lens is approximately 146mm long and weighs a little under 700g.

Canon EF 80-200mm,f/2.8

A further jump in quality gives this lens absolutely exceptional status. The rotary ring allows particularly precise setting. The widest aperture remains the same throughout the focal length range and, together with an image quality designed to satisfy the highest professional demands, allows this lens to be used for all photographic tasks. Three UD elements reduce aberrations, including chromatic faults, to a minimum previously unknown in this focal length range. It is therefore an apochromat and a lens Canon are particularly proud of. The two focusing ranges of 1.8m to infinity and 3.5m to infinity facilitate very fast focusing. The lens is fast enough for focusing even in twilight and in badly-lit rooms. The powerful arch-type motor manages super-fast focusing across the entire range in 0.5 sec.

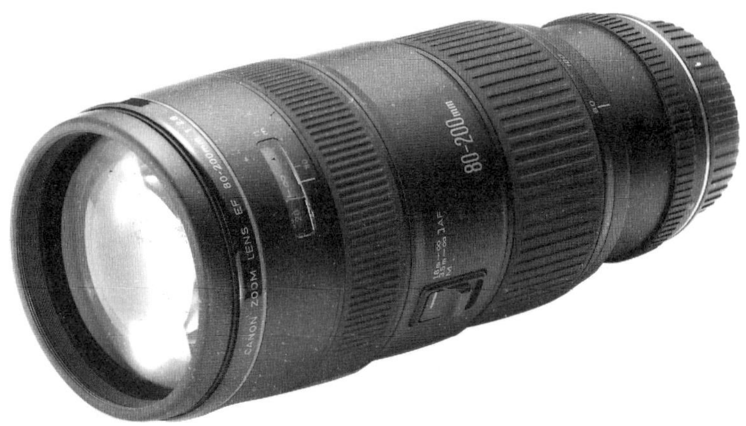

Canon EF 80-200mm,f/2.8 L - high speed for the most popular longer focal lengths.

Canon EF 70-210mm,f/3.5-4.5 USM

This compact lens has a fast internal focusing system. The slide zoom consists of 14 elements in 10 groups. The focusing speed from infinity to 1.5m is just 0.5 sec, and manual focusing is possible without switching off the AF mode.

The smallest subject area is between 45.9x68.9cm and 17.6x26.4cm, and between 35.9x53.9cm and 140x210mm in the macro range. Depending on the selected focal length, the lens is between 121mm and 170mm long. The weight is 550g. This zoom is one of the new lens designs which also feed their distance setting into the camera computer, and therefore influence the control mechanism of the portrait and close-up programs.

Canon EF 100-200mm,f/4.5 A

On this inexpensive lens only the zoom ring can be operated manually. Manual focusing is not possible. Its construction comprises 10 elements in 7 groups. The focusing speed across the entire range is 0.7 sec. The shortest focusing distance is 1.9m and the smallest subject area is between 18.8x27.8cm and 39.4x58.8cm. The lens is 130mm long and weighs 520g.

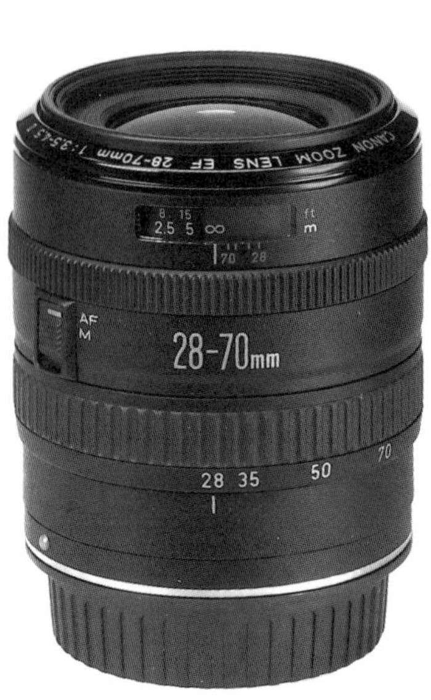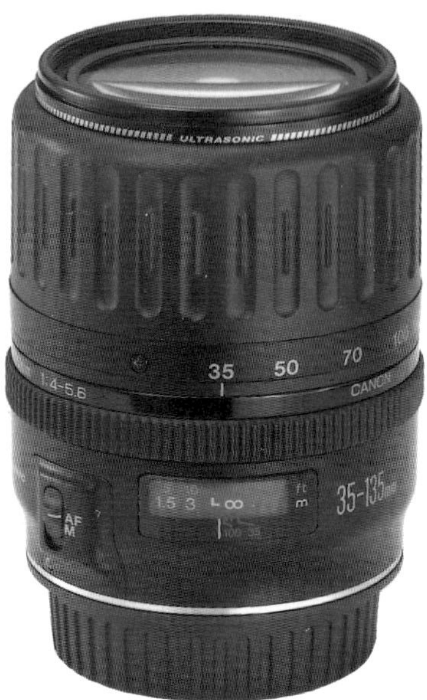

The Canon EF 28-70mm,f/3.5-4.5 II (left) and the EF 70-210mm,f/4 make a very versatile pair. The Canon EF 35-135mm,f/4-5.6 USM (right) - a zoom which is good for many successful shots, even if it is the only lens in your outfit. Because of the ultrasonic motor it is very quiet.

Canon EF 80-200mm,f/2.8 L

Three UD glass elements ensure absolute top quality, and the optical construction consists of 16 elements in 13 groups.

The rotary ring allows particularly precise setting.

The widest aperture remains constant across the entire focal length range. The arch-type motor focuses from infinity to 1.8m in an astonishingly short 0.5 sec. To make this even faster, there is a distance limitation from 3.5m to infinity. At 1.8m distance the smallest subject area is barely postcard-size, exactly 9.4x14.1cm. At the same distance, but with the shortest focal length, the subject area grows to the size of a sheet of typing paper. The lens does not have a macro setting. With a length of 185.7mm it is not extremely small and at 1,330g it is not exactly a lightweight. But this is not to be expected from a top professional lens with a filter size of 72mm.

Canon EF 100-300mm,f/5.6
Canon EF 100-300mm,f/5.6 L

Two lenses with the same construction, but the L quality is achieved with fluorite and UD glass, which maximise performance across the entire focal length range. The optical construction consists of 15 elements in 10 groups in both cases. Focusing speed from infinity to 2m is 0.89 sec. The smallest subject area is between 38.7x58,1cm and 13.3x20cm, and in the macro range between 27x40.4cm and 9.2x13.8cm - smaller than a postcard. Both lenses are just under 17cm long and weigh a little less than 700g.

Canon EF 100-300mm,f/4.5-5.6 USM

This compact lens is just 12cm long and has an optical construction comprising 13 elements in 10 groups. Fast internal focusing guarantees short focusing speeds of 0.5 sec across the whole distance range. Simultaneous manual and automatic focusing is also possible. The shortest focusing distance is 2m, 1.5m in macro mode.

The smallest subject area from 2m is between 43.7x65.5cm and 16.3x24.4cm. In the macro range this is reduced further to between 32x48cm and 12x18cm. This is one of the new USM lenses, which feed the reproduction scale into the camera computer in the portrait and close-up programs. This data is taken into account in the setting of the aperture, thereby controlling the background effect (sharp or unsharp).

Some Specialist Fixed-focus Lenses

Canon Fisheye EF 15mm,f/2.8

This is the Canon lens in the EOS range which always gives you a panoramic view. It has an angle of view of 180° along the diagonal. That corresponds to 137° horizontally.

It is also the only lens which bends the straight lines of a subject, both in the picture and in the viewfinder. Only those lines which run through the centre of the image keep their original shape. Objects of the same size, again ranged parallel to the focal

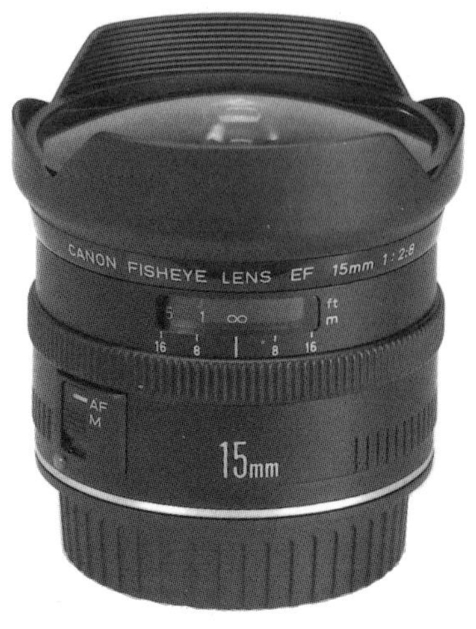

Canon EF 15mm, f/2.8 - a fisheye with a diagonal angle of view of 180°.

plane, become smaller towards the edge of the image, and the degree of curvature becomes stronger. Depth of field behaves according to the same rules.

This strong curvature of straight lines is not distortion in the sense of a fault. The name 'fisheye' means that this is a lens which does not reproduce images according to the laws of central perspective, but that in this case the laws of spherical perspective apply.

If the camera is held exactly vertical for a landscape shot, and the horizon is positioned near the central horizontal line in the viewfinder, this lens creates the effect of a super wide-angle shot, so long as there is nothing clearly structured in the foreground. But as soon as the camera is tilted forward and the horizon slips towards the upper edge of the shot, the subject appears as part of a sphere, a bit like the view of the earth from outer space. If the horizon is moved towards the lower edge of the shot by tilting the camera upwards the horizon bends the other way, running upwards along the edges of the shot.

The Canon EF 15mm fisheye has a shortest focusing distance of 20cm, not to the front of the lens, but to the focal plane. As a consequence of the different type of perspective and the small reproduction scale that goes with it, this focal length has extreme depth of field. This means that you don't even have to choose the minimum aperture of f/22 if everything from a few centimetres away all the way to the horizon is to appear sharp.

The integral lens hood does not allow normal filter fitting. This is why this lens has a special integral filter compartment at the back. Filter foil, preferably special gelatine filters, have to be cut to 31x31mm to slide into this compartment.

This is a fisheye lens with frame-filling reproduction, thanks to 8 elements in 7 groups. The focusing speed of its arch-type motor from infinity to 20cm is exactly 0.36 sec, and the subject area is then just 17.1x25.7cm. The lens is 62.2mm long and weighs 339g.

Canon EF 50mm,f/1 L USM

This lens, announced more than two years ago, has been on the market since late 1989. It has the standard 50mm focal length and the amazing speed of f/1, particularly aimed at professional photographers. It is the fastest of all autofocus SLR lenses currently available. The lens consists of 11 elements in 9 groups,

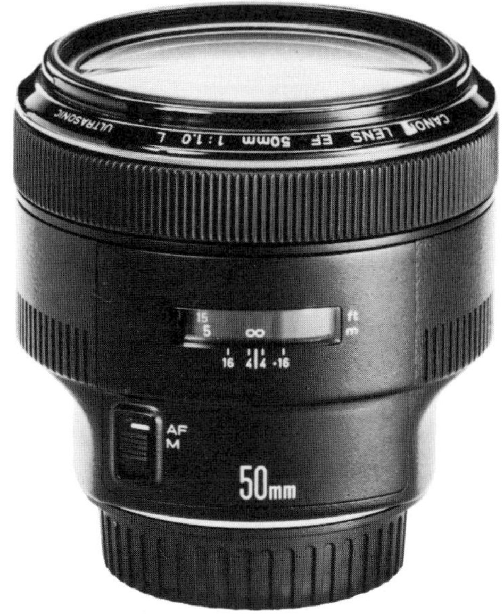

The super-fast Canon EF 50mm,f/1.0 L is a rarity on the world market.

weighing almost 1000g, but without being unwieldy. Two aspherical elements and special glass types with low dispersion - so-called UD glass - are used in the optical system. This gets rid of almost all spherical and colour aberrations. Floating elements correct aberrations, which could cause problems with focus changes, and guarantee high reproduction quality at any focusing distance. This high degree of optical sophistication contributes particularly to the quality of wide aperture shots. This lens is almost two stops faster than the 50mm,f/1.8 lens. In comparison with the EF 85mm,f/1.2, the difference is half a stop, but the price difference is several hundred pounds. Speed and quality in marginal areas certainly have their price.

The focusing distance goes down to 60cm but can and should be taken to the second range, 1m, if the short distance is not essential.

This is the first instance where the work and speed of the USM motor becomes apparent. Experiments in focusing manually from infinity to 60cm always yielded focusing times far longer than when using autofocus. This is not surprising, since the entire focusing process from infinity to the shortest focusing distance takes exactly 1 sec.

Although f/1 is certainly not a necessity for everyone, it can help both keen amateur photographers and professionals cope with plenty of situations and subjects in the most difficult light conditions. At f/1 and 60cm shooting distance the depth of field starts at 59.5cm and ends at 60.3cm; at the largest aperture the infinity range starts at 81m.

The lens is 81.5mm long, has a maximum diameter of 91.5mm and a filter size of 72mm. The smallest subject area, or subject size, at a reproduction scale of 0.11 is 22.8x34.2cm.

Canon EF 85mm,f/1.2 L USM

This professional lens is less than 10cm long, but weighs over a kilo. Focusing with the ultrasonic motor is silent. Thanks to the high speed of f/1.2, the viewfinder image appears extremely bright.

An aspherical element ensures that f/1.2 gives a professional performance and is not just something to brag about. Its charac-

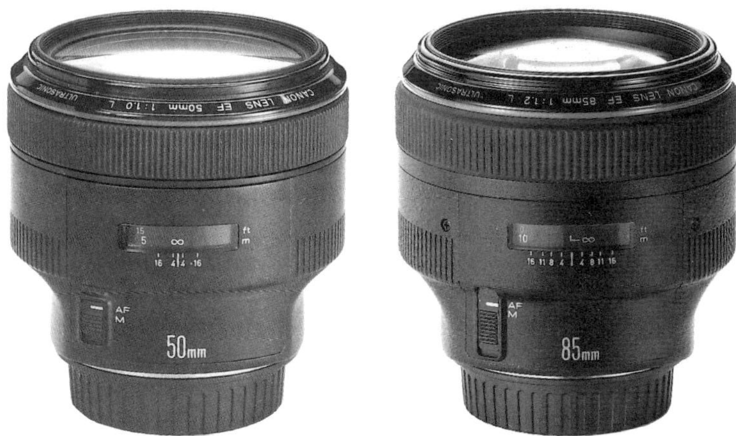

Canon EF 50mm,f/1 L USM and Canon EF 85mm,f/1.2 L USM - incredibly fast, but expensive and really only for 'available light' specialists.

ter will probably appeal to many photographers immediately. While it is considered one of the longer focal length lenses, it does not flatten linear perspective or give a spatial compression of depth. The reproduction scale is increased by a factor of 1.7. This is a very suitable scale for portraits, landscapes and photo journalism. At this speed this lens is suitable for every time of day and almost every time of night. However, the price of this lens could buy you several sets of EOS 1000 equipment.

With this ultra fast portrait lens, 9 elements in 7 groups, including an aspherical lens and floating elements, guarantee high reproduction quality at every distance. The angle of view is 28° 30'. The super-fast ultrasonic motor manages focusing from infinity to 0.95m in 1.2 sec, and manual focusing is available. The smallest subject area is 22.6x33.9cm. The lens is 84mm long, has a diameter of 91.5mm and weighs exactly 1025g.

Specialist Lenses For Things Far Away

Canon EF 200mm,f/1.8 L USM
Canon EF 300mm,f/2.8 L USM
Canon EF 600mm,f/4 L USM

The following three are specialist lenses for professional requirements and special tasks.

The EF 300mm,f/2.8 L was the world's first lens with an ultrasonic motor. By now this has become an exclusive club of ten, with three of them from the same family. As they are different sizes, they don't look like triplets, but otherwise they have much in common. They are first recognized by their completely untypical colour for lenses; grey. All three have an outsize detachable lens hood, a sturdy base with a turning mechanism and tripod socket, as well as two eyelets for a carrying strap of their own. The two smaller ones weigh about three kilos, the larger one six kilos.

But all three of them are something special - dream lenses for everyone whose profession requires them to take photographs with such long focal lengths, or who can afford them for their own amusement.

Optically, the 300mm lens is the successor of the FD 300mm,f/2.8 L, which was enthusiastically received by many professional photographers and became the blueprint for the three grey EOS lenses. Fluorite and UD elements guarantee top performances in contrast and resolution.

With these three lenses the photographer has the opportunity to adapt the automatic focusing method to the photographic task in hand by selecting one of three different focusing speeds.

Step 1 offers half the rotation speed - useful for portrait shots, for example, or subjects in the shorter focusing range, anything which requires precise focusing.

Step 2 works at normal rotation speed.

Step 3 works at double speed - often necessary for sports photography.

A focus memory facility offers user convenience in a class of its own. Regardless of how many other distances were metered in the meantime, a small rotation of the focus ring is enough, and the

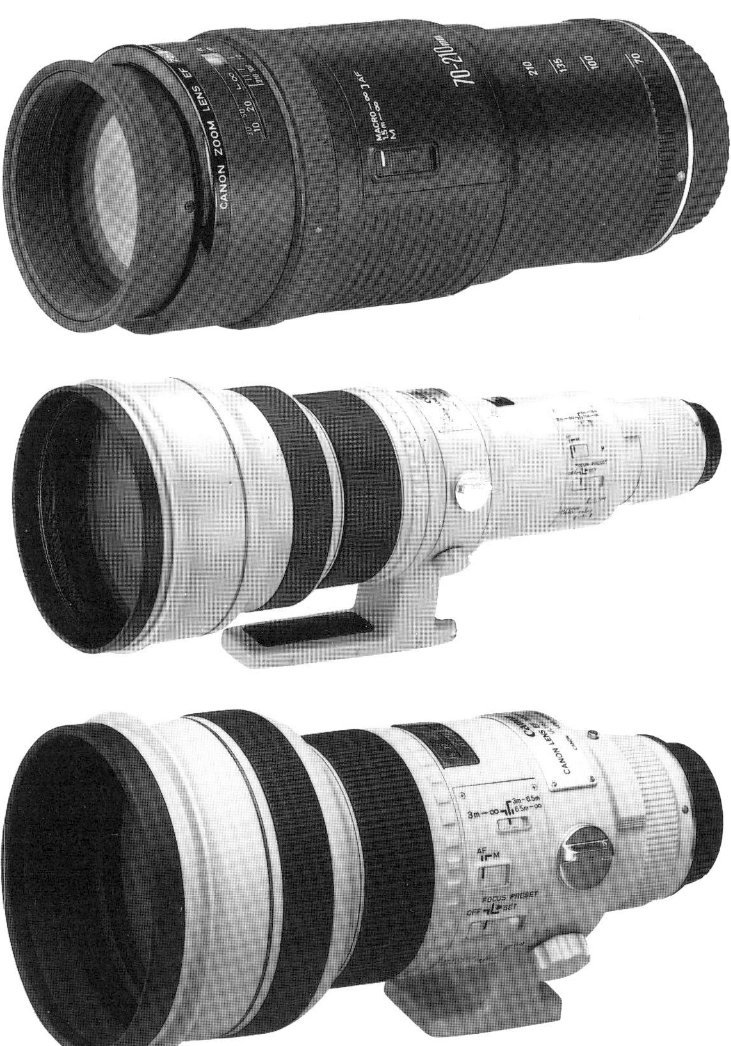

Canon EF 70-210mm, f/4 (top) - a 'classical' tele zoom with a three-fold setting range; the ideal complement to a 28-70mm lens. Canon EF 300mm, f/2.8 L USM (bottom) - ideally suited for all types of action shots; but at least a monopod should relieve the photographer. Canon EF 600mm, f/4 L USM (middle) - ultra-fast super telephoto lens, but not necessarily the right choice for the average consumer.

lens will set the stored data at lightning speed. Sports photographers will particularly appreciate this facility. It enables them to carry on shooting with the second selected shooting distance within a split second, often faster than they can re-align the camera. The process of storing the data is easy and its success is confirmed by an audible signal.

The ultrasonic motor offers electronic power-assisted support for manual focusing; a rotation of the focus ring causes electrical signals which tell the microprocessor of the lens how the ultrasonic motor should run. Manual focusing therefore takes place almost free of vibration.

The focusing distances of telephoto lenses are normally fairly long. Canon has therefore pre-programmed different focusing ranges on all three of these lenses in order to shorten the focusing process wherever possible. There are three pre-set ranges: on the 200mm lens these are 2.5m to infinity, 2.5 to 5m and 5m to infinity. On the 300mm lens they are 3m to infinity, 3m to 6.5m and 6.5m to infinity. On the 600mm telephoto lens the three ranges are 6m to infinity, 6m to 15m and 15m to infinity. The approximate figures are easily remembered if you always start from the minimum distance of one range, taking the focal length as a figure in centimetres, which can then be doubled for the upper limit of the first focusing range. 300mm focal length goes down to a minimum focusing distance of 300cm, and has a focusing range from 300cm to 600cm, 3m to 6m. It is no great tragedy that the actual limit is 6.5m: even if the subject is closer it will be in focus, but if the distance is estimated incorrectly and the subject is too far away, the autofocus will fail and the photographer must quickly adjust the focus manually.

These three lenses are also fitted with a detachable revolving tripod fitting, which facilitates balancing the camera/lens combination on a tripod. It revolves and can be locked in position in 90° steps.

A filter compartment fitted with a clear glass filter is part of the lens construction and allows the use of filters even on these lenses. You can fit a normal 48mm Canon filter, or a circular polarising filter of the same size. A special filter foil attachment is available for red or infrared filters. As these lenses are apochromatically corrected, you will not need a separate IR setting.

The use of a tripod is vital with these lenses. For sports photography or on holiday you should at least have a sturdy monopod, preferably one that is fast to put up and attach. The reason is that it would be a shame if even just a single shot didn't show the full performance these lenses can deliver. As such lens performance is not commonplace even with Canon, I should also mention how much it would cost you to call one of these optical delicacies your own. On the 200mm and 300mm we are talking in terms of over £2,000. For the 600mm lens, including case, you should expect to part with just under £5,000. The 1.4x and 2x extenders developed specifically for these lenses are almost cheap in comparison, even though they are still more expensive than a simple EF 35-70mm zoom lens.

UD glass and particularly the cultivated calcium fluorite crystal, which are protected by a sheet of clear glass at the front of these top quality lenses, are still something unusual. Produced in this extreme size of more than 25cm diameter, they also cost the earth.

The EF 200mm,f/1.8 may appear only for professional use or for special applications in science and technology. An enlargement factor of four compared to a standard lens may not seem very much at a first glance, especially as many zoom lenses provide the same focal length. This first impression appears to be confirmed by a glance at the depth of field at the maximum aperture, providing a sharp zone of only one centimetre at a shooting distance of 2.5m. But let's just take one example; for a sports photographer f/1.8 can determine the success or failure of a job. To capture a Boris Becker serve even remotely in focus an extremely fast shutter speed, the widest possible aperture, and preset focus is needed. Many photo journalists can no longer manage without an EF 200mm,f/1.8, especially if they work for large news agencies or news magazines.

In combination with the special extenders, this lens has a focal length of 300mm and f/2.8; a 2x extender provides 400mm and

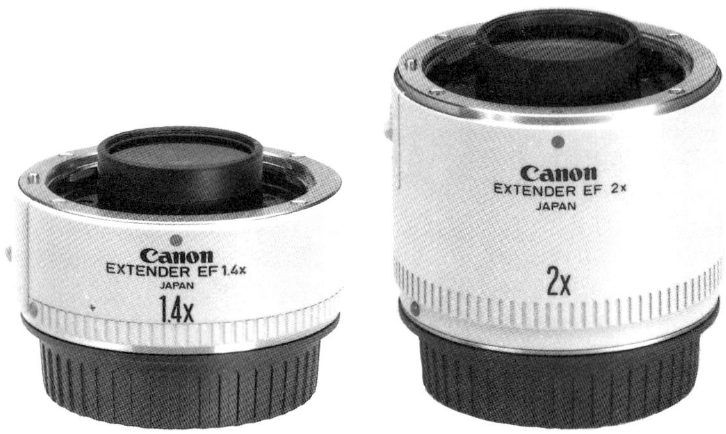

Canon EF 1.4x Extender (left) - turns the EF 600mm,f/4 into an EF 840mm,f/5.6, for example
Canon EF 2x Extender (right) - for the fast 200mm and 300mm lenses in the Canon autofocus range.

f/4.5. The variety of possible subjects is increased greatly with these combinations, and thanks to three UD glasses, the quality does not suffer. These are the reasons why this lens is considered a super telephoto lens; something for specialists as a 200mm lens, as a 300mm or 400mm combination something for professionals, experts and enthusiasts.

The Canon EF 300mm,f/2.8 is the star of many sports arenas and football stadia. For some professional photographers it is a standard lens - standard as far as quality, speed and price are concerned. As focusing is carried out by an ultrasonic motor, it is suitable for stage and theatre photography as well as animal, landscape, sports and press photography. It comes into its own

128

at media events, when photographers are sent into a special press area or behind barriers. With the two extenders it gives focal lengths of 420mm or 600mm and f/4 or f/5.6. It is used for landscapes, expeditions and safaris. Animals can be photographed 6, 8.5 or 12 times as large as with a standard lens. One element made of calcium fluorite and UD glass create the optical conditions for sharpest distance views and a wealth of detail for such unusual subjects.

With the 1.4x extender the Canon EF 600mm, f/4 (the longest focal length in the EOS range) becomes an 840mm, f/5.6 lens. With a 2x extender it goes up to 1200mm and f/8. Animal and some sports photographers, who specialise in surfing or large international sporting events, will use this lens more regularly than many would believe. One calcium fluorite element and two UD elements with anomalous dispersion are necessary in order to eliminate the secondary spectrum. This means that the quality and performance of this lens can compete with all other L lenses. All three Canon super telephoto lenses benefit from super-fast internal focusing which, in combination with the ultrasonic motor, offers extremely fast focusing speeds; 0.6 sec on the 200mm and 300mm, and even with the 600mm it is still under 1 sec - 0.99 sec exactly.

Canon EF 200mm, f/1.8 L USM
Twelve elements in 10 groups, including 3 UD elements and a front protection glass, give an angle of view of 12°. The maximum reproduction scale is 0.088, which corresponds to a subject area of 27.2x40.8cm - the size of a sheet of A3 paper. The lens is 20.8cm long and weighs exactly 3kg.

Canon EF 300mm, f/2.8 L USM
Its optical construction comprises 9 elements in 7 groups, including one fluorite and one UD glass element. This is why, as with the other two, it does not have any chromatic faults or a secondary spectrum. It has an angle of view of 8° 15' and is 25.3cm long. Its weight is 2.855kg. The smallest subject area is 21.8x32.7cm, roughly the size of a sheet of A4 paper.

Canon EF 600mm,f/4 L USM

The optical construction consists of 9 elements in 8 groups, including one fluorite and two UD elements, as well as a front protection glass. It has an angle of view of 4° 15' and the shortest focusing distance of 6m produces a reproduction scale of 0.105x. This corresponds to a subject area of 22.8x34.2cm. The lens is under 50cm long - 456mm exactly. Its maximum diameter is 167mm, and it weighs in at 6kg. All three lenses are supplied with a lens hood, a hard leather case and a lens cap.

For this type of interior shot you need to ensure that the working range of the flashgun (with an ISO/21° film) is between 1 and 4.3m.

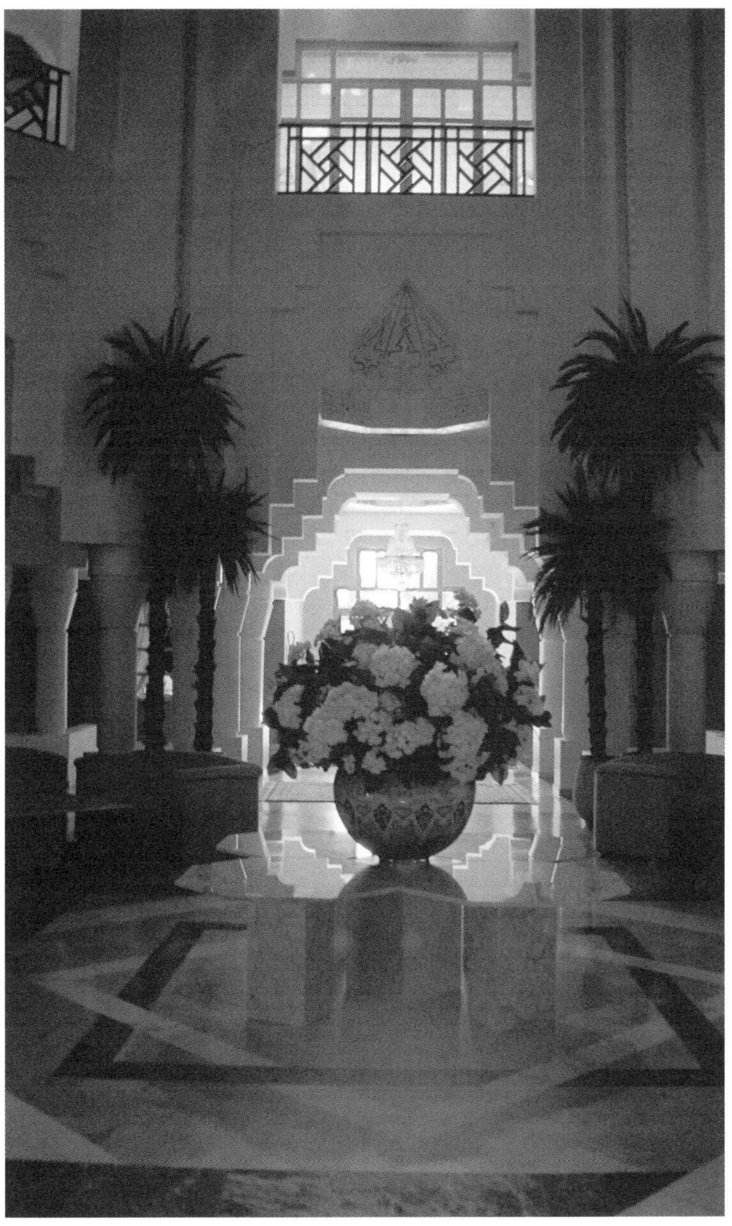

The Flash System

Only the EOS 1000F has an integral fold-out flashgun. It has a guide number of 12 and is controlled by the normal TTL automatic flash system and as soon as it is charged it can flash for any shot in the creative programs. In the subject settings the camera decides whether or not to flash. its coverage angle corresponds to the angle of view of a 35mm wide-angle lens. In adverse light conditions, or when subject contrast is weak, the integral AF auxiliary light aids automatic focusing. The shooting distance range of the automatic flash of the integral flashgun is between 1m and 4.3m when used with an ISO 100/21° film. The x-sync speed of $^1/_{90}$ sec is automatically selected, but you can also select speeds as slow as 30 sec. The recycling time is approx 2 sec, and the flash duration is 1 millisecond or less. The integral flash of the EOS 1000F gets its power from the camera batteries. It works in all exposure modes except the DEP program. However, it is only ever a stop-gap, and an external Canon Speedlite is necessary for really interesting flash techniques, such as automatic fill-in.

External Speedlites from the Canon EOS range are connected to the electronic system of the camera by means of the accessory shoe behind the fold-out flash. The flash techniques described on the following pages refer to flashing with external Canon Speedlites, which can be used both with the EOS 1000 and the EOS 1000F.

The EOS 1000 set already includes the mini-flash Speedlite 200E. This is very compact and runs on four 1.5V AA batteries. It can light the full wide-angle range of the standard zoom lens. With an ISO 100 film the Speedlite 200E has a range of about 5m. The additional figures of 7m (at 35mm) and 5m (at 80mm) apply to shots with colour negative material and make full use of the exposure range of the film. If you use flash with a focal length of

---

Examples of perfectly mastered exposure: the evening mood with the romantic reflection and the silhouetted geese is as much a result of multiple zone metering as the shadow play of the glass at the bottom.

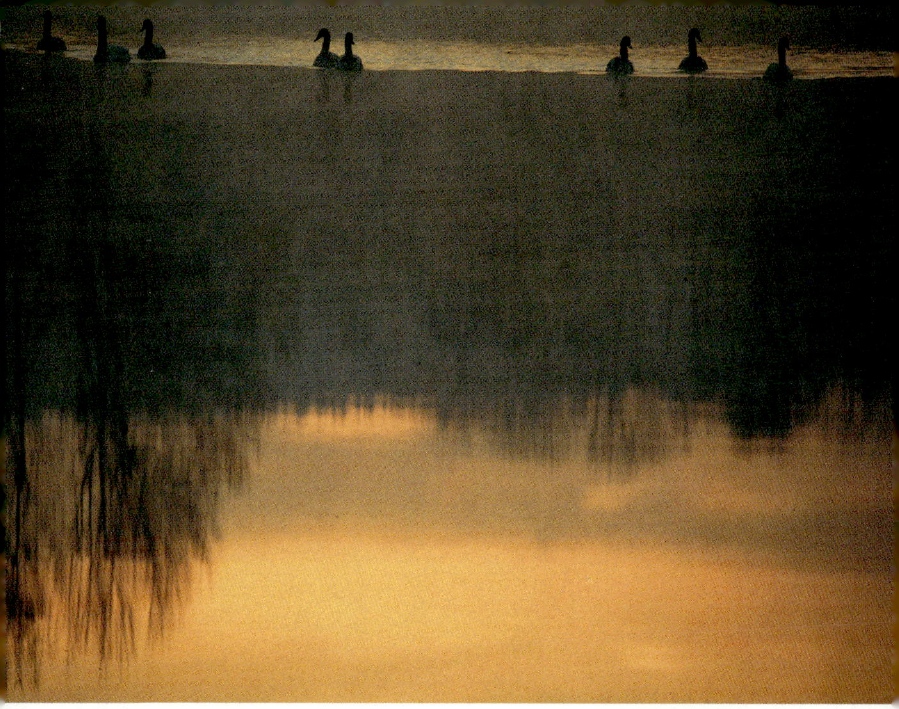

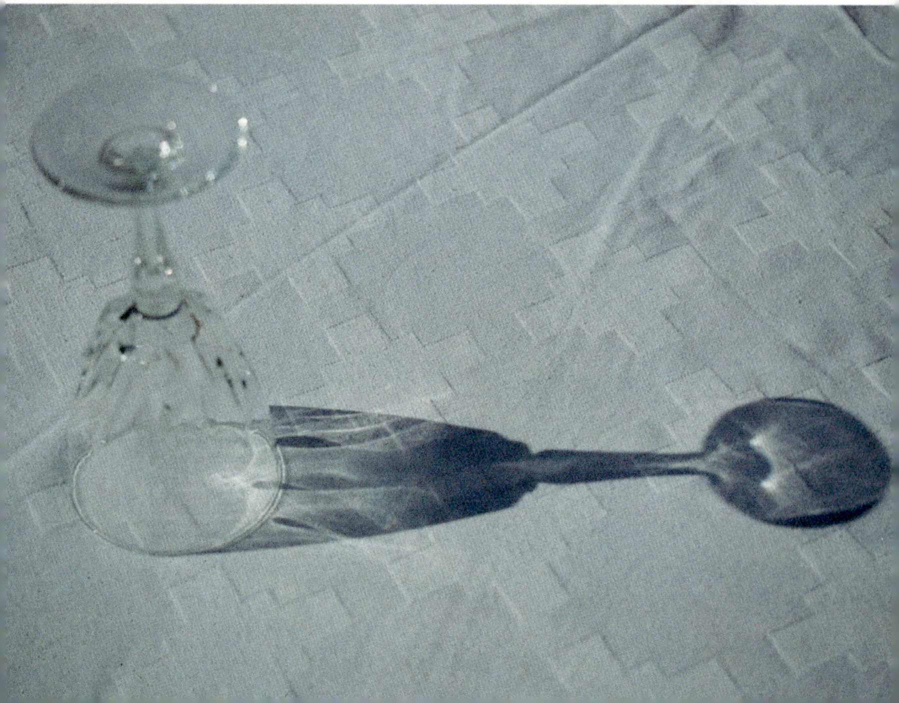

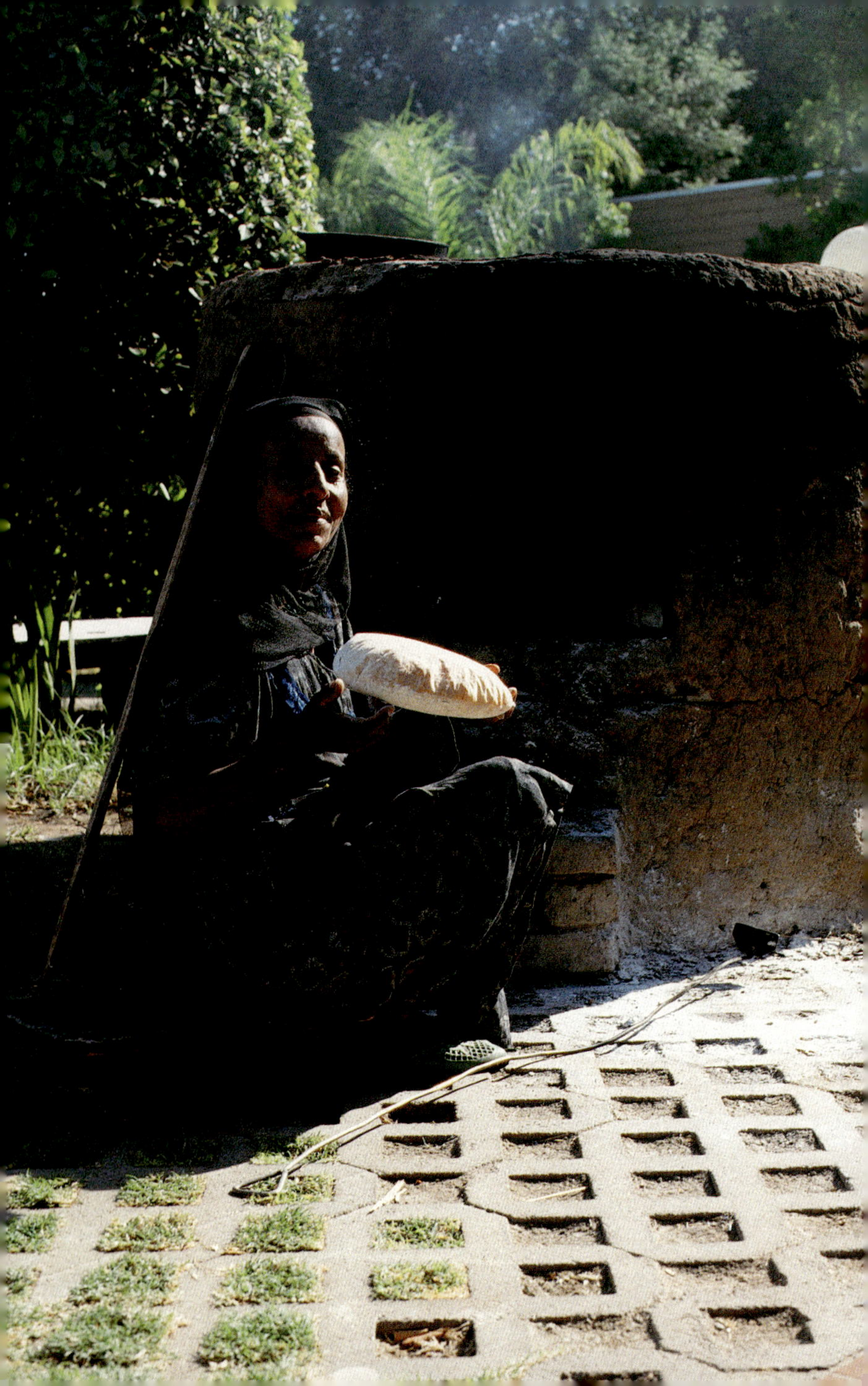

28mm, a diffusion adapter has to be attached to the front of the flash.

It is very important that the flash is locked into position, once attached, by means of the grey switch on the flash itself. Otherwise faulty contact between flash and camera can make nonsense of all your efforts. The flash is ready to shoot when the red LCD on the flash and the flash arrow in the viewfinder are lit continuously. It can then be used in all the P programs, the subject settings, with aperture- or shutter-priority and, of course, in manual mode. Synchronization takes place with the first shutter blind, and if it is too dark for the autofocus, the flash sends an infrared auxiliary light to a distance of about 5m in order to facilitate AF metering. The fastest shutter speed for flash photography - also known as synchronization speed - is $^{1}/_{90}$ sec. In

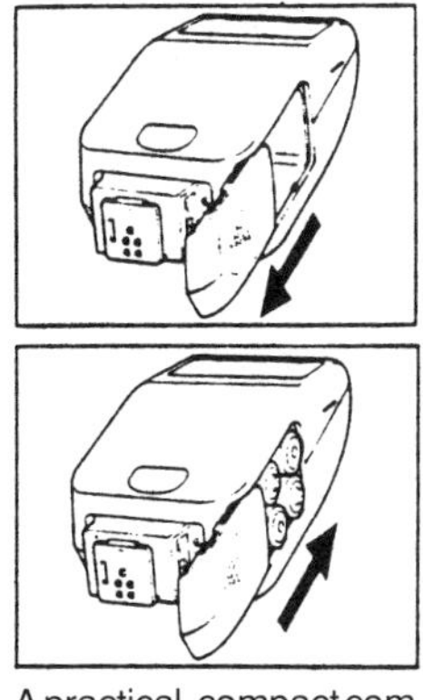

A practical, compact companion for when you are out and about: the Canon Speedlite 200E.

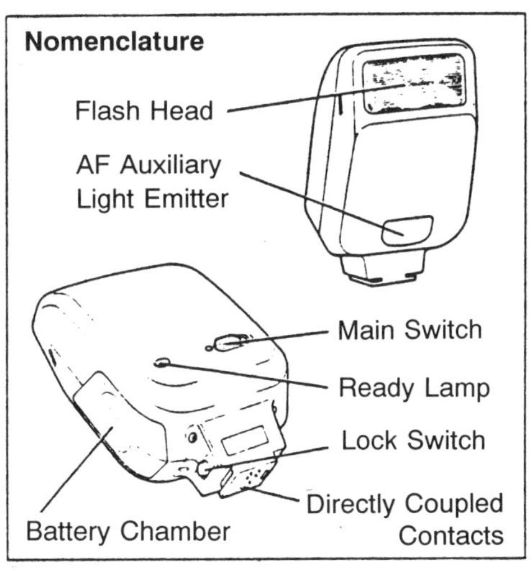

The multiple zone metering system of the Canon EOS 1000 automatically masters difficult light situations with strong contrasts.

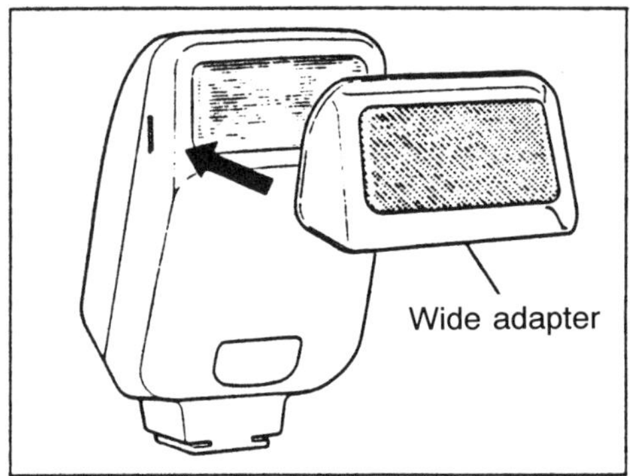

With a wide-angle adapter the flash coverage angle of the Canon Speedlite 200E can be adjusted to the angle of view of a 28mm lens.

ISO	WIDE (35 mm)		TELE (80 mm)	
	Colour print film	Slide film	Color print film	Slide film
100	0.7-7 m 2.3-23 ft	1.0-5 m 3.3-16.4 ft	0.7-5 m 2.3-16.4 ft	0.7-3.6 m 2.3-11.8 ft
400	0.7-14 m 2.3-45.9 ft	1.5-10 m 4.9-33 ft	0.7-10 m 2.3-33 ft	1.5-7 m 4.9-23 ft

shutter-priority mode a slower speed has to be set manually if lighting conditions in a room are to be taken into account. In aperture-priority mode the camera automatically switches to a speed range between 30 and $^1/_{90}$ sec.

Flash Photography in Program Mode

Flash is easiest if everything is set to automatic mode; the lens in autofocus and the camera in 'green zone'. The flash is automatically set to the Canon-specific A-TTL Program. All you have to do is point the AF focus mark at your main subject and watch the green figures and symbols on the lower edge of the image. They will tell you what shutter speed the camera will operate. With the EOS 1000 this can be a minimum of $^1/_{90}$ sec. But it depends on how far the aperture will be closed or opened, and whether the working range of the flash is exceeded. If this is the case, the shutter speed and aperture indicators will flash and request a change of shooting distance.

Fill-in flash: there is no difference in operation, whether you are using the flash as your main light, or filling in. In P mode and all

136

the subject settings the camera will signal that the flash should be switched on by continuous flashing of the flash symbol. In P mode the f/number will start flashing as soon as the EOS Speedlite reaches marginal fill-in values, where ambient light and flash are no longer in the right proportions. This informs you that the background is too light and that the camera will take the light initiative by choosing a shutter speed between $^1/_{60}$ and $^1/_{90}$ sec, because it cannot adapt to the situation by filling in.

Fill-in flash is technically easy to master. But the photographic effect itself and the easily-achieved flash effect won't be everybody's cup of tea. I warmly recommend experimenting, if only to decide which camp you are in, for or against fill-in flash. All backlit subjects are suitable for fill-in flash - whether it's a group shot of the school team, afternoon tea in the garden, or a young foal in the shadow of its mother who is illuminated by backlight. The most beautiful backlighting moods occur early in the morning or in late afternoon, when the sun is low but still quite intense. In this situation fill-in flash can heighten the mood. But that in itself is not the only positive effect. Enlarging or printing in general, and particularly on Cibachrome paper, is simplified substantially because there is more colour in the shadows and the contrast is reduced as a consequence. This means that the effect of shots is often improved quite considerably.

Flash Photography in Shutter-Priority Mode Tv

In Tv mode the photographer selects the shutter speed. This must not be faster than the X-synchronization time, otherwise the negative will have only a part image.

All shutter speeds slower than $^1/_{90}$ sec are suitable for this operating mode of the EOS 1000. When you press the shutter button, the aperture the flash has selected with the help of its auxiliary flash will be displayed in the viewfinder. If the lowest possible f/number is flashing, the background will be too bright despite correct flash lighting. Only a faster shutter speed can help in this case - but only if $^1/_{90}$ sec was not already selected. If the highest f/number is flashing, the main subject is again lit correctly by the flash, but the background will appear too dark. This can be corrected with a slower shutter speed.

It is impossible, at least initially, to remember all programs and their behaviour, let alone their variation in flash mode. That's why, for practical reasons, you should concentrate on one program; flash either in P or Tv mode, and of those two, P is certainly the more convenient.

Flash Photography in Aperture-Priority Mode Av

Many people still hold the opinion that the light of an electronic flash destroys the atmosphere of a shot completely. But this should simply be taken as an indication that people don't know how to use a flash. There are, of course, occasions when it makes sense to reach for a super-fast film and leave the flash alone. But once your eye is trained in the intricacies of lighting conditions, you will recognize certain circumstances even amongst those critical situations, when you can get better photographs - simply more technically-perfect and expressive shots - with a dash of flash.

The way there leads past the automatic flash in aperture-priority mode. Switch your Canon EOS 1000 to Av mode and switch on the attached flash, which has been locked into position. The necessary shutter speed for an aperture of f/5.6 is determined by pressing the shutter button halfway. If another aperture make more sense in the given situation, this should be selected now, and the shutter button should once more be pressed halfway. Flashing green shutter speeds below the viewfinder indicate whether the background will now be too bright or too dark.

The shutter speed automatically selected in Av mode is a result of the total available amount of light. The extra illumination for the area reached by the flash is added to this basic amount of light. It is irrelevant for a technically-perfect flash shot whether the exposure determined in this way is $^1/_{30}$ sec or 30 sec, but in creative terms this makes a lot of difference. The flash can have a fill-in effect or serve as a main light, which can then be used in combination with a slow shutter speed to create special effects. In the first case the existing mood is emphasised; in the second the photographer creates an atmosphere which appears very brilliant through the use of a lighting technique. An everyday situation can provide a simple practical example; a portrait in a living room filled with evening light. In Tv mode the flash will fill the room, the synchronization speed is usually so fast that only flash light is registered. The light in the room is too weak to even leave a trace at $^1/_{90}$ sec. In Av mode the camera first calculates the correct shutter speed for the available light, perhaps $^1/_{30}$ sec, and the mood of the room will come across in the shot.

In this situation the flash only has the task of lighting and filling in the foreground (in this case the portrait) as required by the selected aperture. Everybody will like showing off such a shot, for it reveals a portrait of a person in his or her own surroundings and captures their mood. And this doesn't just work in interiors, but is almost more effective and impressive with exterior shots.

You can, of course, use any of the other Canon Speedlite flashguns in the same situations as the Speedlite 200E.

Accessories and Care for the EOS 1000

Accessories

Grip Extension GR-70

The Canon EOS 1000 is easy to handle even with the standard handgrip, but people with particularly large hands can exchange the standard grip for a GR-70 grip extension with a padded strap.

Filters

If filters such as a UV or skylight filter are to be fitted, it is advisable to attach the lens hood adapter first. You can then fit your filters and finally the lens hood. By the way, it is better to use the lens hood on its own, rather than just a filter without the hood, as this prevents stray light from entering the lens.

The AF system of the EOS 1000 allows only the use of circular polarising filters. Canon themselves offer such filters in the sizes 48mm, 52mm, 58mm and 72mm. However, polarising filters often cause big problems, especially when used with zoom lenses. This is on the one hand because the front element often turns during focusing, and this movement changes the effect achieved by the filter. On the other hand, the front element group of some lenses is moved so far back inside the lens tube that it is not possible to adjust the filter size for some distance and focal length settings. The Cokin filter system has many advantages compared to Canon's own. It offers a large number of adapters and adapter rings to allow filters to be used with EOS EF lenses.

Camera Care

Electronically controlled appliances are particularly sensitive to humidity. If the camera is subjected to severe temperature changes, for example in winter, when it is brought into a warm room from outside, condensation can form on the camera surface. If this happens, the camera should be wiped dry with a cloth.

If it is snowing or raining, the use of a plastic hood, is advisable. For longer stays in areas with high humidity levels the camera should be stored in an airtight metal case, together with a few bags of silica gel which absorbs moisture. But it has to be dried out itself at regular intervals. This is easily done in any oven. Generally the camera should be stored in conditions as cool, dry and free of dust as possible. Avoid prolonged exposure to sunlight. A car boot, glove compartment or rear window are just about the worst possible places to keep a camera. Chemical fumes can also affect the performance of the EOS 1000.

If the camera is not used for a long period of time, film and battery should be removed. Check all functions before you use the camera again in order to avoid any possible disappointments. It is in any case advisable to go through all the functions in the camera manual before you take your camera on holiday. One tip: write the most important program options on a card which you can carry around with you when you are out taking photographs.

Dust brushes with small bellows, widely available from photographic dealers, are the most suitable cleaning implements. The camera body can also be cleaned with a dry cotton cloth, preferably washed several times. Compressed air should be avoided especially inside the camera because it could damage the shutter mechanism or parts of the mirror box. It is possible that the LCD panel may darken in very low temperatures. This is normal and will not affect the camera's functions. As soon as temperatures normalise, the LCD panel will once again be clearly visible. A darkening of the LCD panel can also be due to wear but, according to Canon, this should only happen after about five years. If this is the case, the LCD panel can be replaced by a Canon service agent. Repairs in general should only be carried out by Canon service agents. You can either take your camera to a photographic dealer who will forward it, or directly to a Canon centre.

The Film

As with so many things in life, the choice of a photographic film is a matter of taste. But while you can see what you are buying with a dress or a shirt, you can't see what performance a film will deliver. This is why you have find your ideal film with a bit of experimenting.

The choice of film will primarily depend on the intended purpose. 35mm films can broadly be split into four main groups:
- colour negative films, from which you obtain prints;
- reversal colour films, otherwise known as slide films;
- black-and-white negative films;
- special films, for example: for graphic arts, for special lighting conditions such as infrared, or for technical or scientific application.

With correct processing, slide films produce positive colour pictures 24x36mm in size, showing the natural colours of the subject. The slide is transparent and is normally looked at in a viewer or preferably projected on to a screen. Every slide is unique. Prints can be produced from slides, but in the smaller sizes below 20x28cm they are rarely impressive. Slides are, however, ideal for large-size enlargements. Normal slide films are balanced for daylight and reproduce colours correctly, as long as the lighting still has daylight characteristics.

When you buy a slide film, find out whether processing and perhaps even mounting as slides is included in the price. If processing is included, you will usually receive a despatch envelope so that you can send the film directly to the processing lab. If processing is not included you will need to take the film to a colour lab or a dealer.

A colour negative film produces an image with the complementary colours of the subject. In order to produce a paper print, this image is again exposed on colour paper, either as a contact sheet or in a larger size. In the printing process colours and colour intensity can be influenced by filtering and exposure. As such prints are produced by the thousands every hour, deviations in colour and brightness are inevitable. But how should the machine know that it has just produced a print of a bright red sunset, and not a shot with a red cast? However, colour negative film gives you lots of cheap colour prints of consistent quality. If you print enlargements by hand from your colour negatives, you can improve the colour quality. While slide material is very sensitive to incorrect exposure, negative material is much more tolerant. Even overexposure by two or more stops may not be particularly critical. But if the colour negative film is labelled 'professional', it demands as precise an exposure as possible, which is no problem with the EOS 1000.

Even if you intend to stick to colour negative film, using one or two films to help you get to know and master your camera can be warmly recommended. The reason is simple; a slide shot delivers the result in the exact way the photographer and the camera took it. Possible problems, such as not holding the camera straight or mistakes in exposure, can be recognized immediately. But a spoilt colour print - too little colour or a head that is chopped off - could have happened during printing in the lab. The source of the mistake is not immediately identifiable.

Important criteria for the choice of film are speed and graininess. The film manufacturer tells you how much light is needed for a successful photograph with a particular film by using a standardised scale, called film speed. These days this is expressed on the ISO scale. ISO is short for International Standards Organisation. This scale makes it possible for a Kodacolor Gold colour negative film, produced in the USA, to be sold in Stuttgart, to be exposed in a Japanese camera and to be developed in Cape Town without any problems. All film material produced by all manufacturers worldwide adheres to the same standard.

Film speed therefore tells you how much light is needed to produce a photograph of good quality. A doubling of the ISO figure means a doubling in film speed, and a halving of this figure halves the film speed. A 400 ISO film is twice as fast as 200 ISO material. But it is only a quarter the speed of a 1600 ISO film (400/1600 = 4/16 = 1/4).

Film speed and graininess are related. The finer the grain of the film's light-sensitive silver halide crystals, the finer the grain of the film, and the larger the prints which can be made from it. Generally speaking, the faster the film, the coarser the grain.

Films with a speed between ISO 25 and 50 are called slow. This range comprises the most commonly used speeds for extremely fine-grained high resolution colour films. Slides and negatives can be enlarged to extremely large sizes without noticeable grain and loss of sharpness.

ISO 100 films are considered standard. Colour negative films of ISO 200 are classed nowadays in the same category. These universal films have a fairly fine grain and can be used in many situations. A further advantage is their relatively good tolerance for over- and underexposure. Materials with a speed of ISO 400 are fast and have a discernible grain. But they are ideal for bad light conditions and fast movements, such as in sport. While differences in quality between different manufacturers are not very pronounced in the standard range, this is not the case when we get to ISO 400. On super-fast material, such as ISO 1000 and more, the differences in graininess, sharpness and colour quality are even bigger and dependent on the manufacturing technology. These comments on speed ranges apply to all film materials; colour and black-and-white.

Exposure tolerance is the deviation from the ideal exposure, often expressed in aperture stops, which the film can tolerate without a noticeable loss of quality in the final picture. Slide films generally have a substantially lower exposure latitude than colour negative films. With subjects of extreme contrast these films should be metered with the partial metering option (a star in the viewfinder).

This is not necessary with colour negative material, especially with the evaluative metering method of the EOS 1000, which analyses and considers the light data in the shot.

Because film speed is so important it is often part of the film's name. The name of a Kodak Ektachrome film therefore includes a figure, such as 100, 200 or 400, to give its speed. This film speed figure is also printed clearly on the film package and on the film cassette. DX-coding of 35mm film, initiated and launched by Kodak, has been around since 1983. There are two codes on the film cassette and one on the film itself. A panel of squares, like a chessboard, is located on the film cassette and can be read by modern 35mm cameras. By electronically reading the information on the film cassette, the EOS 1000 receives information about the film's speed and length. This data is primarily important for the exposure metering system, but it also helps the camera's electronics to control the automatic film transport - regardless of whether it is wound back into the cassette as shots are taken, as on the EOS 1000, or whether rewinding takes place after the entire film has been exposed.

The other two codes are intended for the lab, and have resulted in a considerable improvement in the overall standard, particularly of prints. The printers, the fully automatic machines which enlarge the negatives and produce paper prints, can read the bar code on the edge of the colour negative film and can use the data for exposure and correction programs.

Films have only a limited lifespan. This is why a 'use by' date is printed on the film package. If the film is stored in cool, dry conditions, this date can be exceeded by several months without any problems. But once a film has been exposed, it should be processed as quickly as possible in order to avoid any fading of the latent images.

Colour film is the most popular camera material, but black-and-white film is still used in many situations for creative composition. The speed classifications are identical to those in colour photography, but with black-and-white films the photographer is able to use exposure and processing to influence contrast, and the full capabilities of the film speed, to a substantial degree. Black-and-white photography nowadays is more expensive and more complicated than colour photography - inexpensive mass processing is not available.

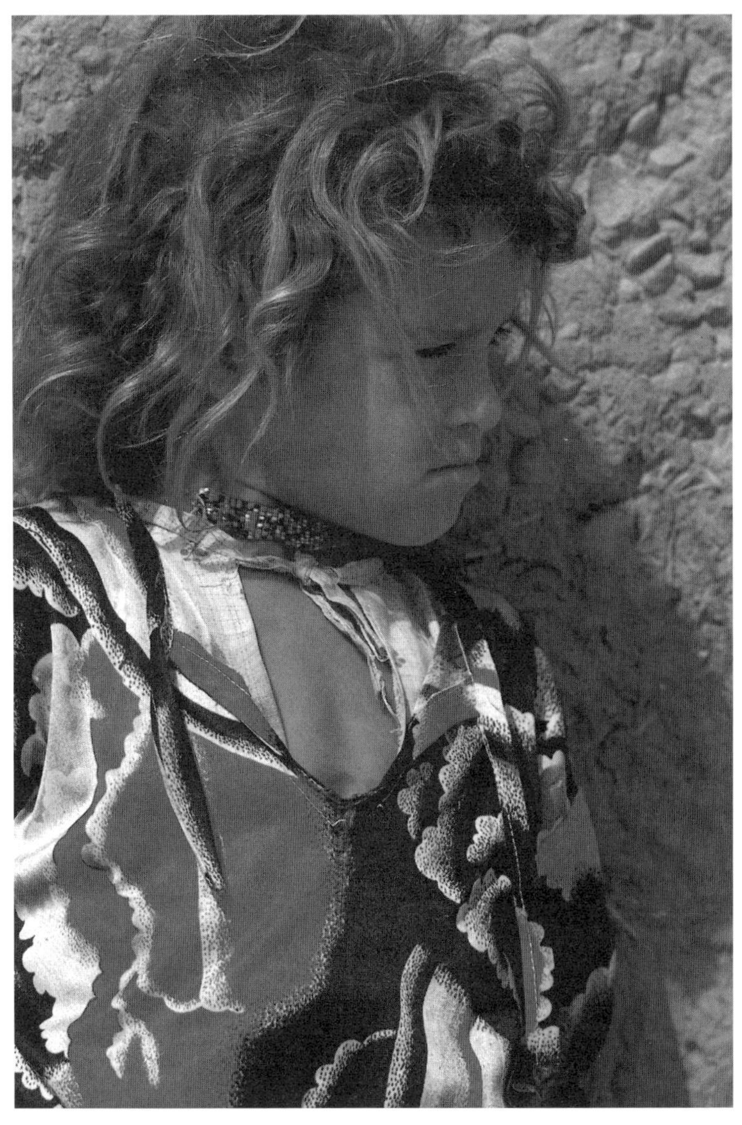

A moderate telephoto focal length and the portrait program help create photographs like this.

Better Photographs with the EOS 1000

Children

Children are an inexhaustible topic, at least for anyone who is a parent or a grandparent. Inexhaustible too are the requirements for film material, because children are captured more frequently in every minute of every day than any other subject. It is a subject most photographers should be experts in. Living photos of a child's free and natural smile are more frequently to be found in our albums today as precious documents and memories than the stilted poses of our youth. This documentation of a child's world and of growing-up is particularly important today, and you should do so consistently for your own children.

You should put as much effort into photographing your children as you put into snapshots and holiday photographs. The more interesting a shot, the more strongly it will remind you of a particular experience, and the more frequently will you reach for the album.

But for good shots you should leave the children in their own world. They don't have to adjust to you, you must adapt to them. You have to recognize their world, learn to see with a child's eyes, or at least from a child's viewpoint - that is, squatting down.

Natural, uninhibited behaviour is the key to the world of child photography. This means firstly that children should become familiar with the camera and with having their photographs taken - it must not become a nuisance or an intrusion. If you want to take good photographs of children you must never forget this golden rule; children should never, ever pose; they must never be 'art-directed' for photographs. Every breach of this rule will make it more difficult for you to get good shots in the future. Natural behaviour also means that the photographer should be familiar with the camera, but with the EOS 1000 this is no problem. With the EOS 1000, photographic technique can be reduced to a minimum to leave you plenty of time for actually taking the photograph. You should be able to handle you camera automatically, in the same way that you can change gears in your car without even thinking about it. If you manage that, you will have plenty of time for perfect snapshots, to make the most of photogenic situations, and quietly to watch the most diverse activities and adventures of your children. For a technically-perfect shot you have to watch several points. But you should never forget one thing; at the decisive moment, when the children's game in front of the camera turns into a series of moments worth photographing, success still depends on the man or woman behind the camera, on the ability to see and to react. At this point the camera should only play a well-functioning supporting role.

In principle you should be able to use any focal length of the EOS system lenses for child photography. But many photographers have problems with wide-angle lenses, because they fit a lot of subject into the frame, even at relatively short shooting distances. You can compensate for this by moving in closer. The smaller reproduction scale also provides a wider depth of field. So the background, which is often an untidy playroom, will appear relatively sharp. But even with exterior shots - on the playground, with a go-cart or a bike - an excessively sharp background can distract from the main subject, your son or daughter.

You have to practise in order to recognize and prevent the intrusion of distracting and unimportant details. Such problems can often be corrected simply by slightly changing your position, or by using your longest focal length, around 200mm. A wide aperture for a subject at about 1m or 2m distance will draw attention to the sharply reproduced subject, and will neutralise the background which will fade into unsharpness. Photographs of children, those which are taken from real life, come alive if they are captured moments. With the EOS 1000 in Av mode and a flashgun you can capture the moods of room and light, simply filling in extra light if necessary. But please don't forget; not even one little shout of encouragement, no posing, no art direction - just watch quietly with the camera and react quickly when you think you could get a good shot. That is how you will get good photographs of children.

Snapshots

For many amateur photographers snapshots are an attempt to get a single presentable photograph by taking lots of harmless shots. The true snapshot demands a sharp eye and perfect control of the camera. There are plenty of snapshot subjects for the amateur photographer; at the funfair, at festivals or sporting events, of people in the countryside or in towns - wherever human beings become the point of interest in a good shot. This also includes comic situations, for example when you see a young couple in front of an advertising poster with a suitable slogan.

Even as an amateur photographer you don't get much time to plan your snapshots, but the EOS 1000 takes care of focusing and exposure metering at lightning speed, so you can concentrate entirely on your subject and on choosing the ideal picture composition. With snapshots you will probably need a lot more film than in normal situations, and you will produce far more shots which are destined for the wastepaper basket. But once you're in the grip of snapshot fever, once you have mastered the art of instantly snatching photo opportunities, you will practise it enthusiastically. But it should be clear that what matters is only the quality of the finished shot, its ability to convey a message to the viewer. The amount of difficulty involved in getting the shot is never a quality criterion. You should always remain polite with your camera, have respect for your human subjects, and think occasionally; would I like to be photographed like this?

In principle, snapshot photography is possible with any lens. But many amateur photographers still believe that only an extremely long focus lens is ideal for snapshots. They completely forget that, in order to get the subject really sharply, the distance has to be set more precisely as the focal length of a lens increases. With the EOS 1000 this isn't a problem. But the longer the focal length, the faster the shutter speed necessary to avoid camera shake blur.

The telephoto effect is often overestimated. Even with a 400mm lens you have to be fairly close to the subject if it is to fill the frame. This means that you have to be as close as 5m for a portrait shot. If you want the whole of the subject in the frame, you can be 20m away from it. This is sufficiently far away to avoid detection with such a giant lens. Almost more important is the effect on perspective, the selective sharpness which separates the different subject planes and therefore helps to remove the usually intrusive effects from the background.

This perspective effect becomes clearly noticeable around the 200mm focal length of the larger EOS 1000 zoom lens, or the same focal length on any of the other zoom lenses. This is a telephoto range which can be used almost everywhere, and without great risk of camera shake.

So how do you get a real telephoto snapshot? It is more a problem of unobtrusive behaviour than one of photographic technique.

The camera should be switched to the sports program. While the light situation allows it, this program places a great deal of emphasis on extremely fast shutter speeds, which reduce the risk of camera shake. If you don't trust this program, you can switch to Av mode and stop down the aperture by one stop. This way you can catch your subjects with minimal depth of field and the fastest possible shutter speed.

You approach the subject without showing any photographic interest. Wait until you have reached the correct shooting distance before you lift the camera to your eye, quickly make sure everything is ready, and then take the picture. Snapshot experience has shown that in many cases there is plenty of time for a second shot. If you are discovered by your subjects, there is only one thing you can do; give them a friendly smile but always ask for their permission. If necessary use sign language, and you will almost always get permission to take your photograph. Discovery is often the end of natural behaviour and spontaneity, but you should always use such an opportunity for a well-composed snapshot or even a frame-filling portrait. You will probably have problems with this method on your first snapshots. Not everybody is good at quickly and naturally lifting the camera, and immediately keeping still so that the shutter button can be pressed. Camera shake is the consequence, part of the price every photographer has to pay for good snapshots.

It means pressing the camera against your forehead and holding the lens from below in such a way that you can press your elbows against your sides. This in itself can reduce the amount of wasted shots by 50%. If at all possible, you should lean against or on something, and you will once again increase your success rate of super-sharp snapshots.

If you are one of those amateur photographers who show respect and politeness for their subject, even in the heat of the moment; if you never try to make someone look ridiculous, then snapshot photography - watching, discovering and quickly reacting to the unexpected - can be a thrilling hobby. You can practise quick snapshots without making a nuisance of yourself in busy pedestrianized areas, at public events, processions, in parks or playing fields. And you would do well to shoot a test film before you try your luck on your annual holiday. Or better still, you can turn your experiments into a great holiday game. Take some 'proper' photographs to show around, and practice taking exciting snapshots with your telephoto lens.

Series and Sequences

Many amateur photographers take two or three shots of important subjects so that they get at least one technically-perfect negative or slide, despite all the risks. Others play with exposure compensation as they would play a piano, in order to get three or five different exposures of this one subject, one of which will then, in their experience, be perfectly lit. Many photographers are happy with this one shot. That's a shame, but you don't have to go into overkill, just to get a single shot. If the subject is worth more than one shot, why not make every one of these a winner, in other words, why not create a series of good shots?

A good single shot is fine, but a small series is almost always better. Photography can only capture one very small slice of time, which is normally measured in hundredths of a second. It doesn't matter whether the subject is static or whether it is a moving scene, as long as the autofocus of the EOS 1000 recognizes this technically important difference. So why should you take three or five identical shots of a single subject?

Why not have a go at shooting in series or short stories, perhaps during a long weekend or on a trip? Your eyes are more prepared to stray from their habitual paths if they are stimulated by new and unusual situations. And this is, of course, why people like to take photographs when they are on holiday. In this situation, encouraged by positive influences, it is very easy to look at things with a photographer's eyes, then everything which is outside the normal daily routine can become a visual experience. As soon as you consciously use this way of seeing, you will start noticing subjects everywhere. Something else is interesting in this type of photography. You don't need any new lenses or gadgets. You just have to change the way you look at things a little. You should always follow that first instinct that tells you 'it's worth it', and spontaneously turn it into a photograph.

Afterwards you can have a closer look at your subject and, if you find further photogenic aspects, you've already got your first series. Wherever you are, you will always notice two or three subject areas fairly quickly, and you should capture them while you can.

It is hard to understand why there are so few amateur photographers who have a pet subject. Yet there are so many examples amongst artists and professional photographers: the old master Kertesz only photographed people for some time, then mirror images for several years. Edward Weston collected shells and small peppers whilst Phillip Halsman asked the most famous people of our century - amongst them Salvador Dali, Marilyn Monroe and Robert Oppenheimer - to jump up into the air in front of his camera. The list is endless and only serves to tell those who complain that everything has already been photographed. There is still photographic virgin territory left!

The subject area you pick is almost irrelevant to start with.

Simply by deciding to concentrate on a subject theme, you will immediately call up information you never normally think about when you take photographs. As soon as you have decided on your theme, you will suddenly look for your subjects with different eyes. The theme is then interesting all over the world, and wherever something suitable crops up in front of you, you will think about taking a photograph of it to improve your series. Think graphically and, above all, get closer to your subject than you would normally. Drastically restricted image sections produce better shapes in the photograph, and colours will develop more of a life of their own.

Subjects Throughout the Year

Spring images: after the grey season of winter the countryside awakens in an explosion of fresh colours, delicate leaves and grasses, buds, and flowers. The extravagant abundance of spring shows in colourful fields and luminous trees. Colourful fields can provide subjects for several rolls of film, from a panorama to a beautiful close-up shot with a telephoto lens. It can be a subject in itself, or an effective backdrop for shots of buzzing bees and small animals, for children picking flowers or running around, for atmospheric, even romantic portraits. This mood is most easily recreated in details, a flowering branch, a single blossom, a frame-filling flower. To do this, the EOS 1000 photographer doesn't need any special equipment. The standard zoom is enough, you can get as close as 37cm. At 80mm focal length your subject area is the size of a postcard. It can be reduced further still with a close-up lens. Don't shy away from using the shortest focusing distance of your lenses for close-up shots. At least try it; the second EOS 1000 zoom lens also delivers thrilling details in the close-up range. The close-up program and automatic focusing reduce the photographic process to recognition and selection of the subject area. The camera's technology almost completely eliminates the main problems of such photographs, camera shake and background intrusion. A good monopod can help further in reducing the danger of camera shake. A monopod is easier to carry around than a tripod, which is certain to be left at home in 99% of the situations where it would be necessary.

Romantic effects are easily achieved with soft focus and are particularly effective if colours glow in the sunshine, or even in backlit conditions. The easiest soft-focus method is still to gently breathe on the lens and then wait for the right degree of soft focus by looking through the viewfinder. A selective soft-focus effect, usually stronger in the centre of the shot, is typical for this breathing method. For backlit shots of blossoms, for example, you can use the Speedlite 200E, which will bring colour and mood into the shot, especially if the background is lighter.

But there's one thing every photographer should get into the habit of doing; a subject which fascinated you enough to take one shot is always worth several. It's better to have a small series of photographs of a beautiful spring subject than to take just a single shot which might not even turn out perfectly.

Summer, Sun and Sunshine

A holiday in the sun should be enjoyed; it should be relaxing and perhaps even exciting. The same goes for holiday photography, and that is easily achieved if you carry your camera around with you at all times. The EOS 1000 with one lens, perhaps even the larger 80-200mm zoom, will be enough.

With the telephoto range set at around 100mm you will probably be able to take frame-filling shots of 80 or 90% of possible subjects.

Your holiday camera can take on two tasks; it is firstly a photographic notebook, fulfilling the role of a diary, and secondly allows you to be creative, and to experiment creatively. On holiday especially you will have the time to play around and experiment with photography.

You have the opportunity to get to know your camera and to lose your fear of all those buttons and switches. That will enable you to use the camera's technology for more expressive shots. Why not try the DEP program to discover the possibilities of depth of field? Have a go when you next take a walk. First focus on the path in front of you, then on the background, and when you press the shutter button halfway for the third time the camera will tell you

---

Colour contrasts used creatively, as in these photographs by Edmund Bugdoll.

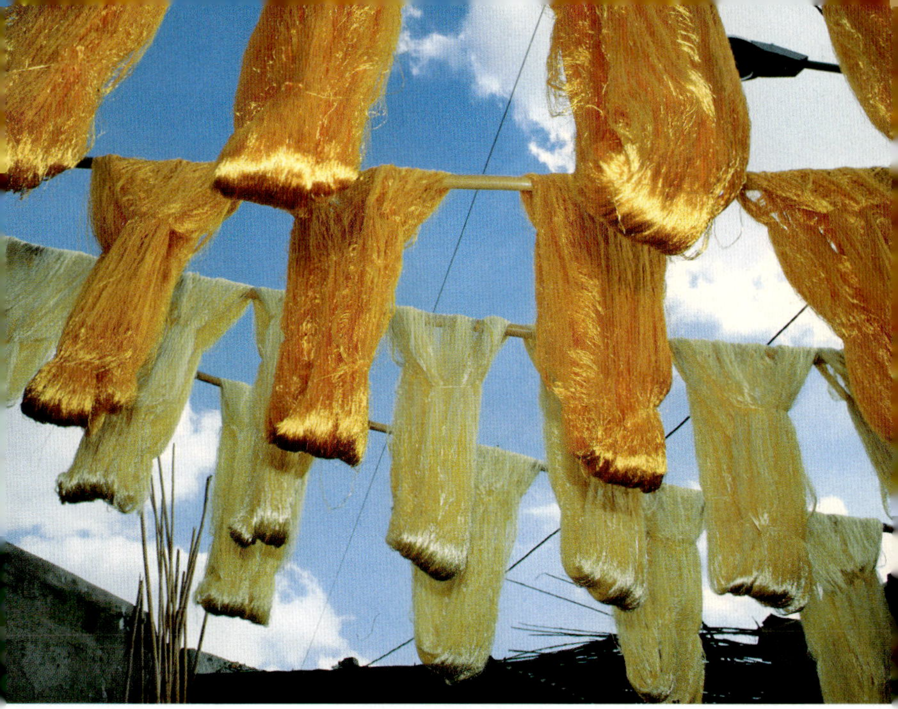

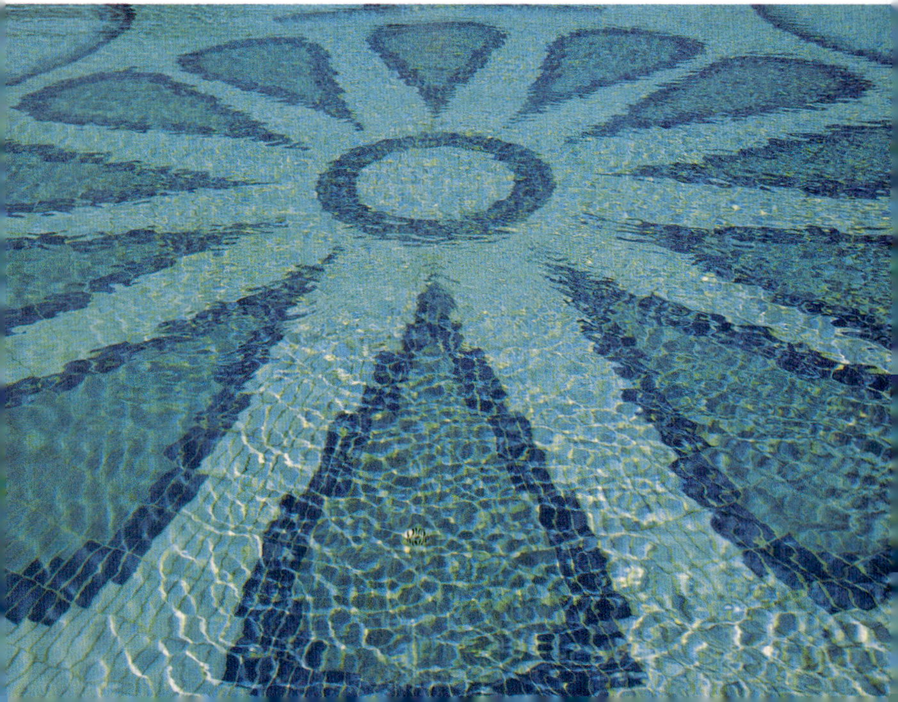

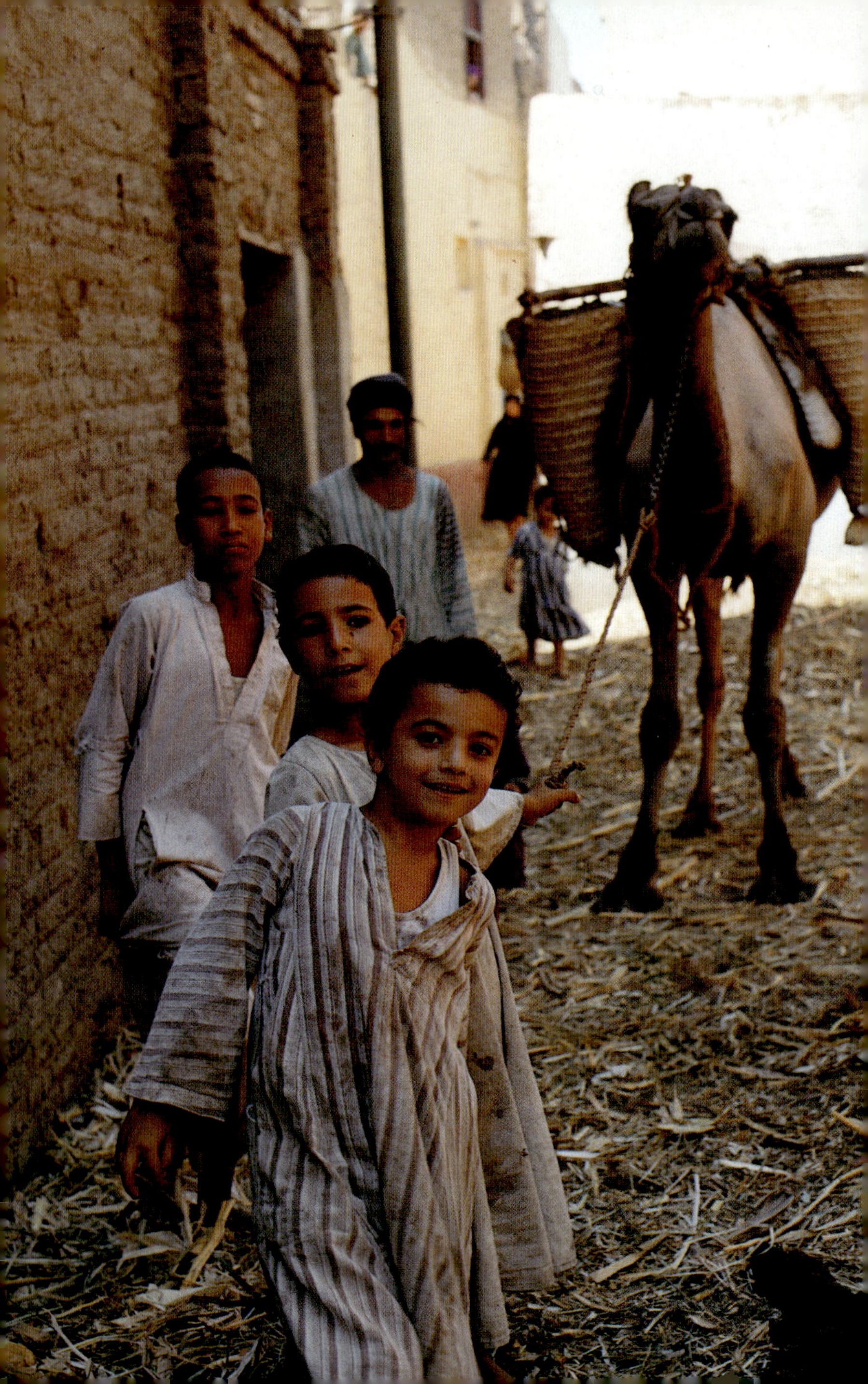

if it's possible. Or you could try to get the village fountain and the background sharp at the same time. Or swans on a lake, with the mountains in the background sharp as well.

If you discover a yellow buttercup, flowering broom, or bright red poppies, you can practise creative picture composition with a single blossom or a twig. Keep the lens set on infinity and hold the flower just a few centimetres in front of the lens. You will see a brightly luminous yellow or red veil in the focus mark, a completely unsharp flower. This is a simple and clever trick for covering a boring foreground with a coloured veil and for making intrusive image details invisible.

You have to make sure that the flower doesn't interfere with focusing, and that you don't stop down by more than one stop. A smaller aperture, such as f/8 or f/11, will turn the flower into an intrusive smudge of colour. In the aperture-priority program, you should select the aperture (otherwise it is always f/5.6 in this program) and then take the shot in automatic mode. This method is guaranteed to help you improve every holiday photograph. This picturesque unsharpness only occurs with a wide open aperture, and the normal viewfinder image and the final result correspond once more.

If you try experiments like this with different focal lengths, you will soon notice that the unsharpness increases with increasing focal length. With a super wide-angle lens the butter-cup has to be placed almost on the front element, at 135mm focal length it can be a good 20-30cm away from the lens.

A low viewpoint emphasises more strongly the foreground of a shot, for example grass and flowers in a field. The main subject can often be detached from an intrusive background in this way, and be shown against a blue sky. You can vary the effect by changing the aperture. The widest aperture delivers the image as seen in the viewfinder. A small aperture, at least f/11 or better still f/16, gives large depth of field, and in the DEP program you can determine precisely how big the zone of sharpness is to be.

Alternatively try the bird's eye view. There's nothing wrong - at least photographically - with looking down on people. You can see more from above. If you use different focal lengths as well, you can further increase the drama of your shots.

Watch Out - Horizon!

No matter from what position you look at a landscape subject, you should always take a second look at the horizon in the viewfinder. A horizon running through the exact centre of a shot, dividing the subject into halves, is always boring. You can emphasise the impression of proximity by moving the horizon towards the top of the viewfinder. If it is close to the bottom of the shot, it emphasises the impression of distance, making the landscape endless. Amateur photographers will rarely have the time and leisure to study the rules of picture composition and to gather their own experience. But it is worth experimenting, and your shots will show that you had fun and enjoyed taking them.

Wonderful Autumn Colours

If you are tempted to go for a walk because it's a sunny late autumn day and the countryside is gloriously colourful, you should never leave your camera behind. The 400g of the EOS 1000 won't make this too much of a chore. Photography as a creative hobby can provide relaxation in the same way that you use a walk to switch off, experience and discover nature and get out in the fresh air. A simple empty slide frame, preferably without glass, is ideal for a relaxing hunt for subjects.

The colours of autumn, which are particularly intense if you have the sun behind you, and in backlit conditions when the sun is low, increase your perceptiveness and make it easier to recognize good subjects. In order to improve your ability to imagine what a shot will look like, you should frequently look through the camera's viewfinder or use the slide frame as a viewer.

Looking through the slide frame makes it easier to choose the ideal image section. If you hold the frame about 5cm away from the eye, you will get the same effect as with a standard lens. Simply try it by looking through the viewfinder and the frame in turn until you get an identical image section. By moving the frame away from, or towards, the eye whilst looking at your subject, you can determine the best possible section and, with a bit of practice, you will be able to determine the desired focal length. But moving the frame away from you to get a smaller section means in this case that you are much too far away from the subject, and that you will get a shot with far too much in it, and that your subject will be reproduced much too small.

By simply changing the distance between frame and eye you can determine the best possible image section in a single hand movement. And this determining of the optimum image section is something which far too often does not happen at all. From a technical point of view, autumn subjects are easily handled with the EOS 1000, at least as long as it is sunny. If you are looking for particularly colourful slide shots, these should still have contrast even in the brightest areas, the highlights, of the shot. Bright areas without details, which show just the clear film in extreme cases, are overexposed. Particularly with backlit subjects it is better to use the partial metering method to control exposure. This exposure compensation is not needed for colour negative films for paper prints, and especially when evaluative metering is used.

Autumn colours don't necessarily mean multi-coloured shots. A single red leaf, or several of them, are certainly effective. But lots of red and yellow leaves together in one shot may be far from restful in a picture. This is why panorama shots in autumn especially demand a lot of concentration.

Close-ups, on the other hand, are generally far more effective, clearly telling a story about the multitude of colour nuances and different colour intensities.

Fairly Foggy

Every amateur photographer who has mastered normal lighting conditions will be able to take sensitive and surprisingly effective shots in bad weather or even in the fog. The difficulty certainly isn't the know-how, but the courage to take photographs, to try something new. It really isn't true that fog can't be photographed because you can't see anything. If your eye can see something, you can also take a photograph. There is quite a lot that can be seen in the fog; for example the way in which contours and shapes appear only as differences of light and shade, and slowly take on colours as they come closer.

Photographically fog is a softener, a romantic, but also dark and threatening, eerie in the darkness. But when white mist rises from a field, when the sun breaks through billowing banks of fog, bringing colours to life - then you're guaranteed to get unusual shots with strong atmospheric effects. With the help of the two EOS 1000 lenses those moods can be intensified or weakened, giving you a wide range of creative opportunities.

The mood of a shot can be increased further if a light source - be it a street light or the misty sun seen against the sky - is used to heighten the contrast, the difference between light and dark. But fog swallows light, a surprisingly large amount of light. This is why faster films should be used; ISO 200/24° for slides, and as fast as ISO 400/27° for colour negative film.

The exposure metering system of the EOS does not have to be adjusted for evaluative metering, but in manual mode you should make a positive exposure compensation. This is what the exposure compensation button at the back of the EOS 1000 is for. A positive compensation allows more light to reach the film, a negative one less. Compensation by +1, that is double the amount of light, is almost always necessary in these circumstances.

You don't need to worry about the camera itself, even in adverse weather conditions. It is fog-proof and can withstand splashes of water. If you want to be extra careful you can protect the front element of your lens with a UV filter. Your own bad weather gear is far more important, you won't enjoy taking photographs in the fog if the cold and damp starts to seep trough your clothes!

Snow and Ice

Snow and ice are photogenic in all weather conditions, but you will get the most beautiful and intense colours in sunshine. If it is snowing you will get monochrome shots with delicate colours with a strong grey tinge. But the snow is hardly ever white. This is not the fault of your EOS 1000, or that of the film you are using. The shot is probably right, but your memory for colours probably isn't. The eye doesn't look too closely at colours it knows or seems to know, and it therefore does not always realise when a colour changes. This may come as a surprise, but snow is very rarely really white - probably only when it is lit by sunlight, and then it glows and sparkles. If it is so bright that you can't look at it without squinting or reaching for your sun-glasses, you should always make an exposure compensation, especially if you're using slide film.

But you should only make a positive compensation to allow more light to reach the film. This may sound astonishing at first, but it is true that bright subjects need generous exposure, and dark ones less, if their mood is to be recreated on film. You can control and influence the degree of reflection by using a circular polarising filter.

Backlighting is the most effective for snow. But there isn't a film which is able to reproduce its sparkle and the huge differences in brightness between light and shade in all their nuances and with a lot of detail in all areas of the shot. A stray black shadow which was deliberately used as black in the shot is no disaster. But the same can't be said of a white area which came out far too light and without any contrast.

Areas of snow appear more three-dimensional in backlit conditions; the play of light and shade quickly conveys a typical winter atmosphere. Skiing, tobogganing and other subjects are surrounded by light auras or reduced to silhouettes. It is therefore best to take shots in front of bright, calm backgrounds. Possible colour casts should be left as they are, at least if you're using slide film - they provide extra atmosphere. The processing lab will attempt to get rid of any colour casts on prints, no matter whether they're deliberate or not.

Colour casts are particularly effective when their origins are obvious to the viewer, as they would be with a sunset. But sometimes it's enough to get the sun indirectly into the shot, to hide it behind a skier or a tree. The sun should only appear directly in the shot if you can look at it with the naked eye.

You should be especially careful in winter not to take too many panorama shots; these will very rarely turn out as you had hoped. White quickly becomes boring and if there isn't enough shadow in the shot to give a three-dimensional effect, you should at least have sufficiently large details at about two or three metres distance. It's worth trying to emphasise perspective in every case. Trees, branches, huts, fences all lend themselves for this purpose. A deep track in the snow always looks good and guides the viewer's eye into the shot. The DEP program is ideal in all these situations; the landscape program is suitable only if used with a wide-angle lens.

The DEP program is also a good technical basis if you want to capture seasonal sporting activities. You can start with digging snow, cross-country or downhill skiing, curling or skating. It is particularly easy if you have agreed with the subject which way the movement is going to take. You can then set your DEP program and simply wait until the subject enters the selected depth of field zone. But as all EOS 1000 lenses have a close-up setting, you shouldn't forget the details. A forgotten autumn leaf with thick cap of snow, a branch with icicles or a fir tree under a pile of snow - they can become attractive subjects. And it doesn't matter whether they'll end up in the album or will be projected on to a large screen. You can often find special offers for big enlargements, especially in January, so the chances of getting a big winter shot to hang on the wall are really quite good.

A Brief EOS Glossary

Accessory Shoe
With central contact and four further contacts to control the functions of Canon Speedlite flashguns.

AF Auxiliary Flash
Canon system flashguns automatically send infrared auxiliary light with a maximum emission at 700nm, activated by the camera as required.

AF Auxiliary Light
This is accommodated in the separate flashgun and activated automatically if required.

AF Focus Mark
A rectangle inside the partial metering area in the viewfinder.

AF Signal
A short beep tone which signals in all programs that focusing has taken place.

AF Switch
A switch on the lens for setting AF (Autofocus) or manual focusing. This is not possible on lenses with the additional 'A' marking. Switching is not necessary on USM lenses.

AF Symbol
The round green LCD indicator in the bottom right-hand corner of the viewfinder. It warns by flashing when focusing cannot take place.

AF System
TTL-SIR (TTL Secondary Image Registration), phase recognition by BASIS (Base-Stored-Image Sensor). AF is activated by press-

ing the shutter button halfway. The AF symbol lights up once focusing has taken place.

Focus lock. Shutter release can only take place after successful focusing.

Manual focusing by turning the manual focusing ring after switching the focus switch to M.

AI Servo

Also called 'dynamic autofocus'. The lens automatically adjusts the sharpness as long as the shooting distance between camera and subject continues to change. Automatic switching between single frame and AI Servo; autofocus operation does not change once AI focus has been activated. As it is also dependent on the motor winder, continuous exposure mode requires AI focus in all cases.

Aperture-Priority

Av; the photographer pre-selects the aperture; otherwise standard setting at f/5.6; the shutter speed is determined automatically, with all metering methods. If there is a danger of underexposure, the 30 sec shutter speed will flash; if overexposure is possible, the $^1/_{1000}$ sec indicator will flash.

Autofocus

The autofocus control system operates by phase recognition using a Base-Stored Image Sensor system. This technique is known as TTL-SIR (TTL-Secondary Image Registration).

Autofocus Lock

By pressing and holding the shutter button halfway.

Autofocus Range

From light value 1 to 18 with ISO 100/21°.

Automatic Program

Program Shift possible in P and self-timer programs; program shift not available in the 'green zone' program.

Battery Check

Takes place automatically when the camera is switched on and shown by a bar diagram in the LCD display. If the battery symbol flashes continuously, the battery needs to be changed.

Battery

One 6V lithium battery in the handgrip.

Battery Life

In normal temperatures and without use of flash, approximately 40, 36-exposure films. In temperatures below 0° the life is reduced considerably, to about 30 films, and even more drastically at temperatures below -20°.

Battery Symbol

Shows the state of the battery in all programs; located in the LCD panel. If only a black area is visible, a replacement battery should be kept ready to be inserted as soon as the symbol disappears completely. A flashing battery symbol in the LCD panel means that the battery should be changed immediately. It can also be a signal for a functional error. In this case press the shutter button; if the flashing symbol disappears, the camera is again working correctly. If it does not disappear after several attempts, there is a defect which should be checked professionally.

B(ulb)

Better known as 'B' or 'bulb', in manual mode if the shutter speed is to be longer than 30 sec.

Cassette Symbol

Indicates on the LCD panel whether a film is loaded and correctly transported.

Central Command Dial

The dial to the left of the viewfinder eyepiece; offers 13 possible settings; camera electrics switched off in the L(ock) setting.

Close-up Shots

A subject setting with single frame operation for the world of
small things; with ONE SHOT AF for the selection of the best
focusing point, partial metering and therefore no background
intrusion; the camera will set moderate apertures while retaining
shutter speeds suitable for hand-held shots. Flash is requested by
flashing symbol.

Depth of Field

The distance in front of and behind the focused plane showing
circles of confusion so small that they still appear as points.
Influenced by the aperture. Depth of field area behind the focusing plane is about twice as long as in front of it. Can be defined
precisely with the DEP program; first metering of the closest
desired focusing point by pressing the shutter button halfway,
second metering of the most distant desired focusing point, again
by pressing the shutter button halfway. The shutter speed and
aperture for the selected depth of field are displayed in the
viewfinder when the shutter button is pressed halfway for the
third time.

Supplementary Eyepiece Lenses

These are available to help short- and long-sighted people see the
viewfinder image clearly. They are available in +3, +2, +1.5, +1,
+0.5, 0, -0.5, -2, -3 and -4 dioptres.

Dioptric Setting

Viewfinder eyepiece adjusted to -1 dioptre (distance to eye:
19.3mm).

DX-Coding

Automatic setting of film speed via a code printed on the film
cassette. Range: between ISO 6 and 6400, in one-third steps.
Manual setting possible with central command dial.

Electronic Command Dial

Conveniently located above the shutter button, this dial is used
for shifting exposure in all the creative programs. The shutter

speed/aperture combination is adjusted to have a longer or shorter shutter speed or a larger or smaller aperture.

Exposure

TTL metering, new evaluative metering method (in all programs), partial metering (by pressing button in P, Av or Tv mode), centre-weighted integral metering (only in M mode), A-TTL flash metering reflected by the film and metered in the mirror box. Positive or negative exposures compensation by up to two EV steps, DX-coding between ISO 25/15° and 5000/38°, manual selection between ISO 6/9° and 6400/36°.

Exposure Compensation Button

Oval button next to the round partial metering button on the back of the camera. If pressed with the thumb, the electronic input dial can be turned to select an exposure compensation (+ or -) of up to 2 EV steps. Once the compensation has been made, the +/- symbol is visible in the viewfinder and LCD panel.

Exposure Metering System

Open aperture integral metering system with SPC (Silicon Photocell). Two metering methods can be selected; evaluative field metering in three zones and partial metering of 9.5% of the subject area in the creative programs (P, Tv, Av, M, DEP and Self-timer). Used with telephoto focal lengths, partial metering almost becomes spot metering; the partial metering button is therefore also know as the spot button.

Exposure Lock

As long as the shutter button is held down, the metered exposure remains stored. This enables shifting to a different image section without changing the exposure. The same applies to partial metering by pressing the button on the back of the camera.

Exposure Programs

1. 'Green zone' standard program (intelligent automatic program)
2. Subject settings: portrait, landscape, close-up, snapshot/sports

3. Automatic program P, identical to the 'green zone' program, but with variable program shift

4. Shutter-priority Tv

5. Aperture-priority Av

6. Manual exposure

7. Depth of field program (DEP)

8. Self-timer program (as P)

9. Flash program (A-TTL automatic flash program and TTL automatic flash program with Canon system flashguns)

Fill-in Flash

Switching on of the attached flashgun for fill-in is requested if there are substantial differences in brightness (more than -3EV steps). If the aperture figure flashes the main subject will be exposed correctly, but the background will be overexposed.

Film Cassette Window

In back of camera.

Film Loading

If the film is pulled out as far as the indicator mark inside the film compartment and the back cover is closed, the film is automatically wound forward to the last frame and is transported back by one frame each time a shot is taken.

Film Rewind

Carried out automatically by the integral micro motor. Is activated after every shot and pulls the exposed piece of film back into the cassette.

Film Speeds

ISO 6/9° to 6400/39° in one-third steps, automatically set according to DX-coding. The same figures can also be selected manually by setting the command dial to ISO and turning the electronic input dial to set the desired speed.

Flash Control Mechanism

TTL flash metering.

Flashgun Speedlite 200E Guide number based on ISO 100 film, recycling time approximately 2 sec.
Flash coverage angle: corresponds to the angle of view of a 35mm lens.
Shooting distance range: 1m to 4.3m based on ISO 100.
Flash duration: 1 ms or less.
Power source: four 1.5V batteries.

Flashguns Speedlite 200, 300, 430EZ
In automatic program: aperture selection is automatic in A-TTL flash mode and with infrared auxiliary light. Automatic selection of X-synchronization speed between $^1/_{60}$ sec and $^1/_{90}$ sec when ready to shoot. TTL-control by metering the light reflected by the film.

Flash Socket
Direct connection via X-contact in accessory shoe.

Focusing Screen
New matt laser screen containing the AF focus mark.

Focus Mark
The focusing mark is visible in the viewfinder of the EOS 1000.

FULL AUTO
The 'green zone' indicates fully automatic operating mode. Focusing, exposure and film transport are carried out automatically, as are flash exposures when a flashgun is attached and switched on.

Fully Automatic Operating Mode
Available by setting the command dial to 'green zone', 'P' or self-timer. Can be used with Canon Speedlite flashguns.

Handgrip
A handgrip extension is available for the EOS 1000. GR-70 extends the normal handgrip and has an adjustable strap.

ISO Speeds
ISO 6/9° to 6400/39°.

Landscape Program
A subject setting specifically designed for wide-angle lenses. Prefers wide depth of field. Single frame operation, three-zone evaluative metering, one-shot AF, focus and exposure lock allow important details to be sharp away from the centre of the shot.

Lens
Standard zoom lens 35-80mm, f/4-5.6; also available: additional zoom lens 80-200mm, f/4.5-5.6, 8cm long, weighing 275g. The 35-80mm zoom consists of 8 elements in 8 groups, is just under 7cm long and weighs 180g; shortest focusing distance 35cm, providing an subject area of 96x144mm (postcard-size).

Lens Connection
Canon EF bayonet with fully automatic data transfer.

Lithium Battery
Wipe battery and camera contacts with a clean cloth before loading the battery.

Manual Exposure Selection
In manual shutter speed and aperture selection mode, the exposure metering system is still active as a back-up. For convenience the middle finger should be used to press the shutter button ; the usually more mobile forefinger can easily select the shutter speed or aperture with the electronic input dial whilst the thumb operates the exposure compensation button. The difference between the selected shutter speed/aperture combination and that chosen by the camera can be seen on the correction bar.

Manual Focusing Ring
For manual focusing of the lens.

Dimensions
148mm (W) x 96.5mm (H) x 68mm (D)

Metering Range

EV 2 to 20 at normal temperatures with 50mm, f/1.4 lens and ISO 100.

M-FOCUS

Can be selected on almost all lenses. The green signal still serves as a focus signal.

Multiple Exposures

For special effects the EOS 1000 allows two or more multiple exposures of the same piece of film to be selected on the electronic input dial. To do this, the partial metering and exposure compensation buttons on the back of the camera have to be pressed simultaneously until 'ME' appears on the LCD panel. The number of multiple exposures can then be programmed with the electronic input dial. The process is set off by pressing the shutter button. The film is automatically wound on when all the multiple exposures have been made. Watch your exposure compensation depending on the number of overlaps. The camera automatically switches back into normal mode.

Multiple Field Metering

A three-zone evaluative metering method new to Canon.

One Shot

Static autofocus particularly suitable for motionless objects. The lens no longer moves after focusing has taken place. Focus and exposure are stored as long as the shutter button remains pressed halfway. The shutter cannot be released if focusing cannot take place.

Operating Elements

LCD panel is switched on for 6 sec when the shutter button is pressed. Partial metering button and exposure compensation button on the back. Pressing both buttons either causes the film to be rewound (remove lens), or allows programming of up to nine multiple exposures (ME) if the electronic input dial is turned at the same time. Inbuilt self-timer with 10 sec running time.

P

The automatic, self-timer and green zone automatic programs have the same features. However, the P and self-timer programs can be influenced by program shift and exposure compensation. The programs are known as 'intelligent' automatic programs because they select the shutter speed depending on the focal length and only begin to release the shutter if the shutter speed is the same as, or shorter than, the reciprocal of the focal length. This also applies to zoom lenses whose focal length is fed into the camera computer. With USM lenses the reproduction scale is also fed into the camera computer. If the flash symbol is flashing, the flashgun should be attached and switched on to fill in or serve as the main light source.

Partial Metering

The metering area corresponds to the circle in the viewfinder, the result is displayed as a star symbol in the viewfinder and can be stored by holding the shutter button halfway down. Works in all creative programs but not the subject settings. The most exact metering method, but takes getting used to.

Partial Metering Button

Button underneath the LCD display at the back of the camera; press firmly with your thumb. Function available in all creative programs, indicated by a star symbol in the viewfinder.

PIC Program

All the subject settings (PIC=Program Image Control).

Polarising Filters

Circular polarising filters required in order to allow correct operation of the exposure metering and autofocus systems. Available in the Canon range. The most important filter of all for removing unwanted reflections. Almost more important for clean colours in landscape shots. Use particularly around noon. Intensifies blue of the sky at right-angles to the sun.

Portrait Program

For shots with short telephoto focal lengths; prefers wide apertures; focus lock by keeping the shutter button pressed halfway is therefore advisable when focusing on the subject's eyes. Single frame autofocus and continuous exposure mode with one shot per second. Evaluative metering.

Power Source

One 6V lithium battery (2CR5).

Programs

Five subject settings (Green zone P, portrait, landscape, sports/snapshot and close-up) and six creative exposure programs: program shift on shutter-priority, aperture-priority, depth of field, manual and self-timer programs. Additional automatic flash program when Speedlite flashgun is attached.

Program Selector Button

The dial on the left hand side at top of the camera, also known as the central command dial. It is used to select any of the camera's programs and for manual film speed setting.

Program Shift

Available by turning the electronic input dial in both P programs, Tv, Av and DEP.

Rewind Button

None. If partially exposed films are to be rewound, remove lens, select ISO mode on command dial and press both buttons below the LCD display on the back of the camera.

Self-timer

Located on the central command dial, has a running speed of 10 sec, indicated by a red flashing light and a beep tone which increases in frequency 2 sec before the shutter is released. The countdown from 10 sec is displayed in the LCD display instead of

the frame number and runs in the same way as the program shift
P program.

Shift
Program shift with the electronic input dial; direct selection of
shutter speed and aperture at constant light value. Only possible
in the creative programs. Not available in flash mode.

Shutter
A vertical focal plane shutter; $^1/_{1000}$ to 30 sec; all shutter speeds
electronically controlled; automatic or manual; X-synchronization speed $^1/_{90}$ sec; AF system with two operating modes; operating mode determined by the subject setting or automatically
switched by the camera system.

Shutter Button
Electromagnetic, can only be released after automatic focusing.
Also operates focus lock. Contact with shutter button starts AF
metering.

Shutter Priority
Tv, selection of shutter speed by the photographer. Standard
setting $^1/_{125}$ sec. Aperture chosen automatically, no direct depth
of field functions. Viewfinder indicators: the largest aperture
flashes if the shot will be underexposed, the smallest if it will be
overexposed.

Slow Shutter Speeds
B(ulb) setting for shutter speeds over 30 sec, for example for
night shots or astronomical shots. The shutter remains open as
long as the shutter button is pressed down. Only available in
manual mode. Turn the electronic input dial until 'Bulb' appears
in the LCD display. If the exposure compensation button on the
back of the camera is pressed as well, the aperture can also be
selected with the electronic input dial.

Snapshots
The sports/snapshot program is useful when photographing with telephoto lenses. Automatic selection of fast shutter speeds with AI Servo and sequence mode.

Speedlite
Canon system flashguns.

Sports
Subject setting for sports photography and snapshots; prefers fast shutter speeds; AI Servo; continuous exposure shooting.

Stand-by Indicator
Stand-by indicator on Speedlite flashguns. As soon as the indicator lights up, the camera automatically switches to flash mode.

Subject Settings
Special automatic programs designed to provide maximum performance for the following subject areas: portrait, close-up, landscape, sports and snapshot

System Flashguns
Canon Speedlites 200E, 430EZ, 300EZ and 160EZ. Also for fill-in flash in daylight. AF auxiliary light for automatic focusing in complete darkness. Electronic flashguns with A-TTL and TTL flash metering systems. Attached with cable-free direct central contact. Exclusive to EOS cameras.

Transport
The camera motor winds on the film. Transport mode (single frame or continuous exposure) is determined by the program.

Tripod Socket
1/4" threaded socket on bottom of camera.

USM
Short for ultrasonic motor; the most modern autofocus method.

Viewfinder
Shows 90° of the actual image. Indicates danger of camera shake, successful focusing, aperture and shutter speed; also a flash symbol which flashes if there is insufficient light and is permanently lit up when the flash is ready to shoot. Aperture and/or shutter speed flash if there is a danger of over- or underexposure.

Warning Signal
If the subject is outside the automatic working range, the aperture and shutter speed will flash in the viewfinder when the shutter button is pressed. The distance indicator will flash if the shooting distance is too small.

X-Synchronization Speed
$^1/_{60}$ to $^1/_{90}$ sec, but all slower speeds can also be used for flashing. 'Green zone' symbol. Gives the green light for fully automatic operation.